CONTENTS

You TQlk I Listen

Healing Through Conversations

Pratima Shrivastav

First Edition 2021

Published by:
EMBASSY BOOK DISTRIBUTORS
120, Great Western Building,
Maharashtra Chamber of Commerce Lane,
Fort, Mumbai 400 023, India
Tel: (+9122) - 26689026, 26689290
Email: info@embassybooks.in
Website: www.embassybooks.in

ISBN: 978-93-89995-56-5

Edited by Sapna Bajaj Sawant

Cover Design by Sonal Churi

Layout and typesetting by Sonal Churi &
Gangaram Dhuri (Brand Soul Creations)

Printed & Bound in India by Thomson Press, Mumbai

Special Thanks: Ratna Srivastava (USA) for editorial and design inputs.

Disclaimer: Since we provide confidentiality to 'speakers', names of characters/situations have been changed. Any resemblance to real life is coincidental.

ACKNOWLEDGEMENTS

"Dare to love yourself as if you were a rainbow
with gold at both ends."
*-Author-Poet Aberjhani, Journey through the
Power of the Rainbow*

I am extremely grateful to the Almighty to be born to exemplary parents who set high emotional, spiritual and moral standards. They not only allowed, but even encouraged me to take the path less travelled. They gave me freedom and allowed me to take risks. They exposed me to unconditional love, immense gratitude and abundance in giving. I am also grateful to them for not inculcating in me a structured discipline, which allowed me to push my boundaries, expect the unexpected and follow the path of soul elevation. I believe that it was not by my own design, but engineered by someone up there, who guided me through the vicissitudes of life.

I feel privileged to belong to the rich legacy of three generations of practising *kriyavans*. Our Gurudev, Paramahansa Hariharanand Giri, Guru bhai and disciple of Paramahansa Yogananda (author

Autobiography of a Yogi, founder of Yogada Satsang Society, USA), initiated all three generations into *kriya yog*: my grandfather, (late) Babu Pyare Mohan Srivastava, advocate, Jaunpur, UP, my father, (late) Prem Mohan Srivastava, IRS, and me.

I am also grateful to the continued blessings from Paramahansa Pragyanandji, who perpetuates his legacy as the chosen one. I believe that the lineage of gurus, right from Mahaavatar Babaji, house-holder Kriya Yogi Lahiri Mahashay, Shri Yukteshwar Giri maharaj and Paramahansa Yoganandji have provided abundant positive energy, and will continue transcending humanity towards a better world order.

I can never be thankful enough to Banaras Hindu University (BHU), my alma mater, for the most wonderful, exhilarating and enriching years spent in Varanasi, the abode of Baba Vishwanath. No words can explain the natural seepage of the rich culture and heritage of the mystic city into one's mind, body and spirit. The Ganges, the temples, the *bhang*, the ghats, especially Dashashwamedh and Manikarnika, are all testimony to the rich heritage of the oldest known city in the world and can transform your soul, if you are receptive.

In hindsight, I am also thankful to all the people who wished me ill, cheated and backstabbed me, broke my heart and fooled me. They have contributed immensely to my growth in this rich and fulfilling journey of life.

I honestly believe that it will not be possible to thank all the visible and invisible people and incidents in my life. But I am indebted to Dr. Rajesh Mohan, M.Sc (Phys), Ph.D, LLB, for planting the seed of the idea to write a book I am also thankful to Rajendar Menen, the yogi, writer and editor, for his guidance, Sapna Bajaj Sawant who on-boarded as an editor but embraced the manuscript wholeheartedly and adopted it as her own, and my newfound, lifelong friends Sohin Lakhani and Aruna Joshi.

I believe that God planted the situations and people in my life to achieve what HE wanted me to. My Gurus guided me to the path I needed to take. I just chose the path and walked it sincerely.

INTRODUCTION

"In my early professional years, I was asking the question: How can I treat, or cure, or change this person? Now I would phrase the question in this way: How can I provide a relationship which this person may use for his own personal growth?"
- Carl R. Rogers

As a Corporate Consultant, I have lived in and travelled to many parts of the world. It was a great journey, enriching and fulfilling.

During this period, I have witnessed the emotional trauma of people: of those displaced by war as refugees; of families torn apart during natural disasters, losing all their possessions to nature's fury; of those depending on and being exploited by unfair political systems that left them bereft. In this desperate quest for survival, there was no space or time for emotional enrichment.

We, as a society, are holding back our vulnerabilities to maintain the social image of being happy, confident and complete. In this culture of instant gratification and impatient life structures, emotions have become the first casualty. Emotional issues are often overlooked, and sometimes fleetingly addressed. The need for external support is dire today, more than ever.

While the world strides forward with unprecedented technological advancement, the human race has, paradoxically, never been as miserable as it is in these times. It has never been so confused, directionless, lost and unhappy.

We seem poised now for a Tech-Human interface. Computers have altered our lives irrevocably. New food, new technologies, new medications and new viruses; and an entirely new man is seeking to beckon immortality. The pace is frenetic, and the pressure to "keep up" high.

With the onslaught of machines, new technologies and AI, along with future technologies in the pipeline, man's own inherent capabilities are getting impacted in an irreversible trap. Gadget dependence as a way of life will limit usage of the brain in the future generations, which will be detrimental to brain growth. What if the mechanical robotic generations of the future develop an emotion alien to human understanding. How would that be addressed? Can the order of the universe be changed to a completely different narrative? Time alone will be the real witness.

Despite all the advancements, a mere virus has brought the world to its knees, and we are forced to acknowledge the unquestionable supremacy of the Universe over man and machine.

The speed at which COVID-19 spread, and the casualties thereof, was unprecedented. It swept across all boundaries of caste, creed, community, language and country. It brought humanity on par, sparing no one. No amount of wealth or power could save you from the sly, fast-mutating coronavirus.

Loss and grief felt amputated as bodies of COVID-19 positive victims were not handed over to their families, and cremations/ funerals were performed by unknown hands. The trauma of not being able to say a final goodbye, to accord dignity to our loved ones and perform the rites we believe aid them in their onward journey, all added to the distress.

A major requirement of the human psyche is to be heard, understood and validated. Large families provided an 'emotional buffer' in situations where two involved parties were unable to resolve their issues. With the collapse of the 'joint family system' and the advent of 'double income families', a lot of 'listening' got lost in transition.

The need arose therefore, for a non-judgemental 'listener', who would allow you to vent, to refresh your mind and emotions of all the stress and turmoil, just as one would cleanse one's body every day of all the dust and grime.

HalloHappiness is a safe, secure, confidential platform for emotional health and holistic well-being. Born from a deep desire to look at happiness seriously - not just as a term, but as an honest feel, the platform provides 'listening' to anyone who wishes to 'speak' to someone, ensuring confidentiality. We act only as emotional first-aid, believing that it heals to talk and to be heard. We practice evidence-based counselling and do not prescribe any medication or prescription drug.

At *HalloHappiness*, it is our endeavour to provide you the simple tools, unique to your body and mind, to keep common mental health issues at bay. The idea is to work as a preventive measure. We act as the necessary motivation in times of distress and insurmountable emotional turmoil and provide the 20 percent initial, essential emotional investment to trigger your well being.

I dream of a world full of listeners, providing that emotional cushion for happiness. A world full of consideration, empathy, purpose and the adaptability to reinvent.

Human beings are born with the ability to heal themselves, physically and emotionally. We attach a lot of importance to physical healing. If you cut or burn your finger, it will heal. We don't realise that the same thing happens with our emotions. If your heart is broken, it will heal too. The difference lies in our response. The ability to unlock the strength inherent in human beings, the power to self-heal, lies within us.

Ready to unlock it?

THE BATTLE
OF THE LIVING OLD

OLD AGE BLUES

"Hope is sweet.
Hope is illumining.
Hope is fulfilling.
Hope can be everlasting.
Therefore, do not give up hope,
Even in the sunset of your life."
*- **Sri Chinmoy**, My Life's Soul-Journey: Daily Meditations For
Ever-Increasing Spiritual Fulfillment*

Mr. and Mrs. Bhatia spent most of their life in Dubai, and after 35 years, finally decided to settle down in Mumbai. Their two sons and daughter were educated, married and resided in different parts of the world; the sons in the United States, and the daughter in Australia. Mrs. Bhatia passed away a few years after they relocated to India. She died peacefully of old age.

But much before that, a permanent structure of 'caretaking' was seriously explored and provided for by the children, who ensured that their parents would lack for nothing. Since all of them were living distant from each other, the exercise was undertaken in great detail. Options were explored, and the necessary precautions were taken to appoint the right candidate as domestic help. Given the high incidence of robberies and murders in the city, due diligence was a necessity.

Mrs. Bhatia was my client for a few years and would discuss with me her apprehensions and fears of relocation. There were other issues too which she was not comfortable sharing with her husband. She would voice them, and I would assuage her fears. The relocation was hard; she had left her friends and familiar environment behind, and needed emotional support from time to time to cope with the challenges of a new life.

Meeting with the children was also an issue. Her husband was averse to the lengthy travel involved, although she was fine visiting them wherever they lived. He was keen that they come to Mumbai, which, he argued, would also help the grandchildren connect with their Indian roots. After some deliberation, she agreed.

After his wife passed away, Mr. Bhatia solicited our services frequently. He was lonely and found it difficult to cope. Though he had a good caretaker, he felt the need to reach out.

Sometime in January 2020, he called us to help him with a medical issue and was soon shifted to a hospital. The doctor's worst fears were confirmed. He needed immediate brain surgery.

That was the first time I came in contact with his caretaker Raghu, a young lad from a remote village in Madhya Pradesh. He had been with the couple for close to eight years and loved them dearly. He was at hand when Mrs. Bhatia died and now, was the sole attendant to her husband. He would cater to all his needs, take him to the hospital, and procure and administer the prescribed medication. Since he was the sole caretaker, the doctors explained to Raghu that a signed consent form was a pre-requisite to the surgery. He quickly organised conference calls with the children, who, in turn, immediately arranged the paperwork.

The children pointed out, quite emphatically, that money was not an issue and that their father should receive the best medical treatment available. They also informed that they couldn't be physically present during the surgery but would fly down as soon as they could, given their demanding jobs and time challenges. Since it was an emergency, surgery couldn't be deferred, but it was difficult for them to be in India on such short notice. The surgery was successful, and Mr. Bhatia was discharged from the hospital after the mandatory recovery period.

While convalescing at home, Mr. Bhatia seemed to lose the will to live. He reiterated to us that at the age of 85, with no wife and children around for emotional support, he should be allowed to leave his body peacefully, with dignity. His children's insistence that life was too precious to be thrown away could not convince him. Earlier too, he had been resistant to undergo surgery, but had given in, on the persistence of the children. His point was that he was too old and frail, and would like to leave his body without much ado.

We were in touch with the children all along. We informed them about their father's recovery process and his fragile emotional state. Mr. Bhatia was lonely and his children's presence would have definitely lifted his spirits. We urged them to visit as soon as they could. Thankfully, Raghu was extremely conscientious and devoted, and Mr. Bhatia would often acknowledge him as his 'only son'.

With time, Mr. Bhatia's physical and emotional deterioration was visible. He would justify the delay in his children visiting him and would often say, "Life is much tougher there and they have to do all their work themselves. Not to mention the stress of holding on to jobs these days." He was also worried that his daughter had the added responsibility of the home and children. He wanted them with him, but he understood their predicament.

Then COVID-19 happened. At *HalloHappiness*, it was hectic. We were buried under distress calls. After a month, I received a call from Raghu, who informed me, between sobs, that Mr. Bhatia had passed away and had been cremated with some difficulty, considering the COVID-19 restrictions imposed by the authorities.

Since I had noticed Raghu's attachment to the Bhatias, I was keen to know how he was faring. Raghu had returned to his village. Mr. Bhatia's children weren't comfortable with him staying in the apartment all by himself and had promised to call him whenever they visited India, and to reward him for his unfailing services to their parents for over eight years.

But Raghu was not willing to return to Mumbai. "They should have come to meet their father," he said teary-eyed. "He waited for them but never complained. What is the use of giving me anything? They should have given him that last happiness he so longed for." He reminisced, "When I took up the job, I had no idea what it would entail, but my heart was filled with love for the old couple in the first meeting itself. They were *Bhagwan ke bande* (God's own people) and treated me like their own child. In so many years of living with them, I never had to ask for anything as they were very caring. In return I could only love them as I would my own parents."

I was interested in knowing his future plans as he was a devoted and sincere chap, and a lot of elderly people in a big, uncaring city like Mumbai, could benefit from his services. I could have easily found him work. He rejected my offer saying, "I have an ailing and handicapped father in the village. I took up this job to provide for my father's medical needs. Maybe it is God's design to fulfil my father's desire for his son to spend time with him, which I couldn't all these years due to my monetary needs. Now I will stay and look after him."

Learnings:

1. Dislocation and relocation for the elderly is one of the biggest emotional challenges, especially if they do not have any children living with them. They singularly miss the emotional support and bonding of family. What keeps them going is hope, and something to look forward to.

2. Loneliness and depression are invariably the fallout in this situation. Systematic support should be created to fill the emotional void. We, as a society, have failed here by not catering to this need of the elderly.

3. Keeping busy, interacting with similar age groups, a hobby/ engagement of some kind, yoga and access to spirituality are some of the options recommended. The elderly are generally stuck in their ways and tend to ignore seemingly good advice. Motivation, with emotional support, is necessary to overcome this resistance.

4. It requires a strong will and a desire to live to incorporate our suggestions. We, as counsellors, try to bridge that void. But it is always a challenge.

LONELINESS, A TERMINAL ILLNESS

"Courage doesn't always roar. Sometimes courage is the quiet voice at the end of the day, saying, 'I will try again tomorrow.'"
- Mary Anne Radmacher

Generally, people do not dwell on topics like their own mortality but waste their lives worrying about matters of little consequence. If you were aware of your mortality, you would truly live every moment and probably never postpone things like that much-desired phone call, dancing in the rain or spending quality time with loved ones. While some do not address the subject of death, others fear it and refuse to acknowledge the inevitable. Yes, there are a few aspects of life we have control over, but certainly not the end. No one knows with any certainty how or when they will go. It will perhaps forever remain a mystery.

Sarada, a cancer survivor, is in her twilight years. She was married at a very young age but lost her husband within a few years. Her husband was much older than her and not in the best of health. They had no children.

From an aristocratic family in the North-East of India, Sarada made Mumbai her home for long spells after the detection of her illness. She wanted to avail the best treatment possible, and Mumbai had the top cancer hospital in the country. She would go through her chemotherapy sessions and then travel back home to Meghalaya until her next cycle of treatment. If needed, she would also visit Mumbai for medical consultations. So she would be in and out of the city on a regular basis.

Since Sarada did not know anyone in Mumbai with whom she could stay, she bought a small apartment in the vicinity of the hospital. She also brought two maids along to tend to her, as she could afford it. "I don't know how much time I have. So why not live well until the end?" she stated matter-of-factly. Since she didn't have family or friends in the city, the need to have someone to talk to had to be addressed. She was introduced to *HalloHappiness* by one of the social workers who was assisting her.

In her first call to us, Sarada was full of complaints. She couldn't understand why and how people lived in such a claustrophobic, concrete jungle. She raved about the beauty of Meghalaya, and it was evident that she desperately missed home.

Lalita, one of her older maids, was with her from the time she got married. She was delighted that we were engaged by her mistress. "Didi complains the whole day and we can't change anything for her. Now she can talk to you for hours on the phone. This is a great relief for us." Lalita was happy as we had taken the pressure off her.

Sarada would talk for hours about her home in Meghalaya. She told us how she had lived by herself for many years and managed to keep her assets safe and secure from the land mafia, who had at first approached her as buyers, but when she refused to part with her property, had tried to grab it by force. "Why should I sell to them? People like them are a disgrace to society. Why should I support them? Tomorrow, they will become so powerful that they will dictate terms to simple, innocent people and harass them. At least I can fight. So I don't give in," she asserted with conviction.

When COVID-19 and the lockdown happened, Sarada panicked. It affected her treatment schedule as well as her frequent flights back home. Since she was stranded, she started calling us more often; several times a day, in fact.

She spoke a lot about the past. But we were in for a surprise when Sarada confessed sheepishly that she had a fairly large family (unlike the impression she had given us), but didn't trust anyone. She believed that most of her family wanted to grab her assets. This included her brothers, sisters, nephews and nieces. Her talkative help, Lalita, also filled us in about Sarada's behaviour with the family. But, according to Lalita, her family was not as bad as made out to be.

"Didi's family tried to help her and used to come to her house to spend time, but Didi would shoo them off, sometimes blaming them for lost objects in the house," revealed Lalita. "Once she threatened to file a police complaint and then on, her relatives started to keep away. Her family is not that badly off as to want to usurp her property, but Didi wants to believe that she is very rich and the others are very poor." We urged Lalita to be more sympathetic to her Didi as she was suffering from a terminal disease. But Lalita maintained that her mistress had always been very foul-tempered and difficult to handle. "She has to be happy with herself before she can make others happy, no?" was her retort.

At *HalloHappiness* we tried our best to steer Sarada towards greater positivity. We told her about people who had suffered much more in life and how they had overcome their challenges with a smile. But at 70, Sarada showed little inclination to change. Prolonged emotion of any kind, especially bitterness, can change your persona to one of chronic negativity. Sarada had fallen into the negativity spiral.

Undoubtedly, Sarada's life had been tough, what with an early marriage to a much older man, his sickness and premature death and the subsequent loneliness. She was unable to accept her punctured destiny. "If I had a child, maybe things could have been a little different. I have lived all my life as a lonely woman with no one to really share things with. How does a person survive emotionally? After all that HE has put me through, I am now spending the last years of my life fighting the most dreaded disease. I often feel depressed as there is no sense of belonging with another human being. Both my maids have become a part of my life but it's not the same thing as having someone of your own, like a husband, a son or daughter. However fond we may be of each other, they will still remain the hired help."

She felt lonely but had inherent resilience in living her life on her own terms. She seemed unsettled and complaining sometimes, but not unhappy, and with her tongue-in-cheek humour she could entertain anyone. She treated her maids like sisters as she had no secrets from them and could depend on them for her life.

Sometimes, Sarada would humour me. "If I had found you 40 years ago, I would have been a different person. I always find your positivity very encouraging and keep thinking of our conversations for hours after every call." I kept telling her that there is no age bar for changing oneself. One day she called me out of the blue and said, "You know, only a miracle will change me now. If I get some positive news, it may change me." I tried to explain to her that positivity is within you, it has nothing to do with outside factors, and one can overcome any hurdle in life with that belief. Her approach towards life began changing, albeit slowly.

Sarada continues with her treatment and flies home often. She continues with her lament of being lonely. What will be her undoing: cancer or loneliness?

It is anyone's guess.

Learnings:

1. The dictionary meaning of loneliness is being without company; cut off from others; sad from being alone. Mother Teresa described loneliness and the feeling of being unwanted as 'the most terrible poverty'. Quote: "There are many in the world who are dying for a piece of bread, but there are many more dying for a little love." Impersonal, urban life is eating up an alienated, ageing and lonely population.

2. When one is lonely, powerful emotions can get triggered, like dejection and depression. In extreme cases, loneliness can lead to early death. The immune system gets compromised and the body may host chronic diseases. Loneliness can start eating you from within. It can result in suicide.

3. Everyone feels a little lonely now and again, and medical experts believe that this forlornness can actually be a good thing as long as it is fleeting.

4. Loneliness can lead to rise in our stress hormone levels resulting in fractured sleep, an important factor which repairs our body from daily wear and tear. This might compromise our immune system leading to frequent viral infections, and make us prone to some diseases.

5. Loneliness is normally associated with old age, when one spouse is no more and the children have flown the nest. Intoxicants and other sources of inebriation may help in the short-term, but cause more damage. There is need for more old age homes, and possibly an old age pension scheme, to keep the home fires burning. Economic well-being is not a panacea, but helps.

6. Loneliness in youth is generally an indulgence, but again, a costly one. Psychiatrists and counsellors have a major role to play here.

7. It is important to cultivate a wide range of interests and maybe join some groups one has emotional and physical affiliations with. Recourse to spirituality and religion always helps.

8. Loneliness is rising as an epidemic world-over. UK and Japan have appointed Ministries of Loneliness, while other countries like Germany and Canada may follow suit. UAE has a Ministry of Happiness.

OLD AGE, ISOLATION AND DESPAIR

"Wrinkles should merely indicate where smiles have been."
- Mark Twain

Neeta and Geeta were two sisters aged 69 and 72 years respectively (at the time they approached us). They never married and lived together in a posh suburb of Mumbai. Pursuing a successful corporate career, Neeta had travelled all over the world and lived in various countries, before she decided to come back home to Mumbai for good.

While working in the USA, Neeta was advised to apply for a green card, which she did without much hope. In the 1980s it was a coveted achievement to get a green card; it took years and one had to be blessed. If you were lucky you could also get it under a lottery system, a scheme unique to the USA. Neeta did get lucky and received her green card through the lucky draw. She became eligible for pension and then returned to India. Under the law of pension eligibility, Neeta had to spend 180 days a year in the USA, which she followed diligently. She rented a room with a friend in Florida, where she had lived and worked for many years while residing in America.

"It is quite exciting to live in western countries when one is young," Neeta reflected. "The freedom, rewards of hard work, efficiency, the rule of law and several other conveniences are available, but when you get older, a certain emotional connect is essential, which you can get only in your own country. I wanted to live in the comfort of India and that's what I am doing now," she asserted. "At this age you need support staff. I have slogged all my life to be comfortable in my old age. Yes, things have changed here too, but people are still warm, friendly and respectful to elders."

Geeta, the older sister, taught in a school in Kanpur. After her retirement, she decided to relocate to Mumbai and live with her younger sister. This way, she didn't have to invest in another house and both of them would have each other for company. With their savings, and Neeta's retirement benefits in American dollars, they made a comfortable home for themselves. Although they were not very close emotionally, this arrangement was practical. They had a younger brother who was no more, but his family was around as an extended support system. So it seemed sensible to live in the city where they had grown up.

Besides, both the sisters had health issues and living in Mumbai suited them as medical facilities were top-class and easily accessible. Plus, they could afford the best. Most people settle in Mumbai for its excellent infrastructure. The cost of living is high but if you can afford it, Mumbai has it all. Geeta suffered from diabetes and needed proper management and some medical support from time to time. "I don't need dialysis now but I may need it soon, considering my eating habits and lack of physical activity," she joked.

Both Neeta and Geeta have been living together for seven years now. While they have got used to one another, some differences have also surfaced and sharpened. "With the passing of years, we are becoming intolerant of each other's idiosyncrasies," admits Neeta. Sometimes they end up fighting and don't talk to each other for days. "Our communication remains limited to TV shows," she adds laughingly. "But this is the best arrangement in the circumstances. In old age you need support, and nothing is better than having a family member around." They sometimes wonder what will happen when one of them is no more. "We will cross that bridge then," says Neeta pragmatically.

She has lived in western countries and visited several old age homes. "The biggest tragedy of life is to live in that situation in your twilight years," Neeta shudders. "We have domestic help, a part-time cook, cleaner and a home delivery system here, which is excellent. Everything is available at one's doorstep."

Once a month, the two sisters head out to Pune, Panchgani, Lonavala, Khandala, or some such exotic locale close by. "We love the change of scene," they chorus. "It keeps us happy." They also enjoy the gossip and drama of the neighbourhood. It adds a spark to their mundane lives.

When the pandemic struck, followed by the lockdown, life for the sisters turned topsy-turvy. Suddenly, everything came to a standstill and to make matters worse, they started facing health issues. Even though the health sector was classified as an essential service during the lockdown, it was impossible to travel to any hospital during a medical emergency, as transportation was a challenge. Moreover, once the COVID-19 numbers started increasing, it was impossible to get a bed in a hospital, or even find a doctor. Some hospitals were designated solely for COVID-19 patients and did not entertain patients with other morbidities or ailments.

It was difficult to understand their issues when they called *HalloHappiness* since both spoke together, at the top of their voices. "How can they do this?" they said indignantly. "Don't they know the percentage of senior citizens in this city? How are we supposed to manage without regular supplies? No help is available to do even the small daily chores." Their complaints were numerous and unending.

"There has been no proper cleaning in the house for more than two months now. Is that not important to avoid corona? Hygiene and cleanliness are very important but how do we achieve that? We managed to get someone to give us food. What do we do if we have a medical emergency and there is no conveyance available? The ambulance refuses to take anyone other than a patient suffering from corona. We were hiring cabs for our limited outings. Now even those are not available. Living by yourself in old age is stressful. But now we are seriously depressed and see no light at the end of the tunnel." The sisters were despondent and desperately needed help.

We tried our best to make them look at the positive side. During our long telephone conversations, we shared stories of war heroes who survived on hope, through long years of captivity, before they were finally released. We advised them to treat the onslaught of the pandemic with some equanimity, assured them that the virus would leave as suddenly as it appeared, and that life would be back to normal.

Both Neeta and Geeta were negative and self-defeating. "How do you know that the virus will leave us soon?" they countered. "We have lost all confidence in ourselves, not having stepped out of the house for months."

To keep their idle minds occupied, and to save them from fanciful thoughts, we engaged them in writing a book on recipes. Neeta was widely travelled and had a taste for international cuisines, being a good cook herself. Luckily, they were enthused by the idea. It gave them the most desired ingredient for a content life – being occupied with what they loved! Over a period of time we realised that the project had attracted the involvement of a good number of seniors in their neighbourhood, friends and family.

It made us ponder the effects of loneliness, anxiety, uncertainty and loss of confidence, which could be such a lethal cocktail in the minds of the elderly. In our workshops on 'HOPE', we emphasise on the importance of optimism and the anticipation of a positive future, citing incidents where people have overcome insurmountable challenges, both in war and peace.

Learnings:

1. There is very little that has been done for the elderly, either by law or by way of friendly support.

2. It is important that issues such as these be discussed by involving all the stakeholders, and a roadmap developed for them, to have not only a comfortable life, but also one charged with enthusiasm and hope.

3. With better food habits, medication and an improved quality of life, longevity has been achieved. But a life without engagement or hope, particularly for the elderly, is not a pleasurable experience.

4. The pandemic has highlighted the serious lacunae in the Public Healthcare System which need to be addressed soon.

CHILDREN, PROPERTY AND OLD AGE WOES

"Play with life, laugh with life,
dance lightly with life,
and smile at the riddles of life,
knowing that life's only true lessons are writ small in the margin."
- Jonathan Lockwood Huie

With longevity on the rise, thanks to better nutrition, health awareness and holistic wellbeing, senior citizens today are remarkably fit and sharp. Most of them are in robust health, capable of taking care of household chores, cooking and looking after grandchildren and are committed to varied fitness regimes including brisk walking, marathon running, scuba diving, professional body building or extreme sports. Even those leading sedentary lives have a social network that keeps them busy. Sixty-five is the new 55.

Anjana was born and brought up in Mumbai, got married, had children and went through the usual motions of surviving the city life. In one of her initial calls to *HalloHappiness* she revealed that she was a teacher before she got married. But having two sons in quick succession, she had settled into a life of domesticity and did not have time for anything else. Life was good until tragedy struck and she lost her husband to a sudden, short illness. She was only 55 years old! She came to terms with her fate philosophically: "Who knows what destiny has in store?"

Both her sons were now grown up. The elder one, Vishal, 28, was employed, while Vikas, the younger one, was doing his final year in computer science. They lived in a two-bedroom apartment bought by their father. Life was comfortable.

"I was proud of my children and always boasted about their values, love and affection for each other, and for us," confided Anjana.

"Since our family was not large, we managed well. There was harmony and bonhomie. Then I decided to get my sons married, as it was the right time for them to start a family."

It came as a surprise when Vishal, the elder and quieter of the two, disclosed that he was in a relationship with a colleague. "I had no objection to his choice of partner and he married Aparna. I was happy that I didn't have to go through the rigours of finding a bride for him. I also didn't want to object and put him through further emotional trauma, as he had recently lost his father. The marriage went off well and we were happy."

"Meanwhile, Vikas got a good job and I decided to fulfil my obligation and responsibility to get him settled too," recalled Anjana. "But looking back, I now feel that we may have been hasty, as Vineeta, his wife, was a little forward for our kind of family. Her father was financially better off than us, but they fell for Vikas's good looks and smart personality." Anjana admitted, "Between my two sons, Vikas was always the crowd puller. He used his charm to get what he wanted, even if his demands were sometimes unreasonable."

Anjana recreated the post marriage domestic scenario. "Both my sons and their wives lived with me in the two-bedroom apartment. I gave the boys the bedrooms and shifted to the hall. Alas, marriages are made in heaven but broken on earth. It soon became evident that there was trouble in paradise, but we hoped time would help things settle down. Soon the daily arguments and disharmony started taking a toll on all of us. I was often caught between the fireworks, but felt helpless. Peace became an alien word in the house, arguments took centre stage."

They realised that shortage of personal space was the main cause for the disruption of peace. As Vishal and Aparna were both working professionals, they opted to buy another home for themselves with a bank loan. It wasn't easy, considering the preposterous realty rates in the city.

"By the grace of *Ganpati Bappa*, Vishal could secure an apartment in the same compound as ours, which was a blessing," Anjana recounted. "Vikas, Vineeta and I continued to live together. When Vishal and Aparna shifted to their new apartment, I got back my earlier room." She sounded happy.

Anjana called us again a few days later to report that domestic issues had still not settled down. Vikas had asked Vishal to share their mother's expenses. He pointed out that since his wife was not working, he had the additional burden of catering to her material demands. These conversations continued for a while and came to a head when both of them could not agree on where their mother should live and which son should bear the expenses.

"For the first time in my life I realised I had no identity of my own," confessed Anjana. "First, I was somebody's daughter, then someone's wife and now the mother of two boys, but sadly, there wasn't any Anjana."

Anjana continued calling us. "There has been a lot of yelling and telephonic altercations between the brothers," she reported. "The apartment bought by my husband is my property. It is in my name. Friends and family are advising me to sell it or throw the boys out and disinherit them. But tell me what will I do if my family is not with me? My boys are all the family I have, and I really look forward to a peaceful, fulfilling old age with children and grandchildren."

It's a strange paradox when an elderly parent is just wanting love and the children are only looking for material gain. As a result, Anjana lost emotional security and the desire to live. "I was the proud mother of two boys and wished well for all of us. But that seems like a distant past," she cried.

Her frequent calls were testimony to her emotional trauma. We counselled her to dwell on the happier moments of her life. This was the only way to regain confidence. We also encouraged her to have a talk with her boys and work out a long-term solution. If required, to be firm about disinheriting them, for a peaceful old age. Just the threat may do the job, and sanity may prevail.

She took our advice and initiated several rounds of discussions with her sons. Her animated acceptance was our reward. Things have settled now after Anjana took the boys in confidence and both agreed that she would continue to stay with Vikas, while Vishal would share her expenses.

Learnings:

1. In India, under the joint family system, the elderly were given due respect and attention. However, the emergence of the nuclear family structure has wrought deep cracks at the emotional level.

2. Unfortunately, not much has been done collectively, and individually, to strengthen their own ability to address their feelings of distress.

3. With all the restrictions imposed on them, many elderly persons sometimes lose their self-confidence and the desire to live.

4. The vulnerability of this segment of society requires a dedicated support team to assist them in a crisis. Mental health experts, geriatric care workers (not too many of them are available) and other healthcare professionals are needed to provide the cushion.

5. A dedicated helpline and a systematic daily contact mechanism are the need of the hour.

6. Most elderly people are unable to cope with emotionally demanding situations and probably don't have much to fall back upon financially. Their situation is particularly grave if they haven't saved money or have not subscribed to any pension scheme. Then they become dependent on their children, if they have any, or are forced to live hand to mouth.

   Contrastingly, those who own properties constantly feel insecure and threatened with children vying for and waiting for the inheritance to pass on. Parents should clearly define their assets and fairly divide them among their children so there is no bad blood later. This way they can spend the rest of their days in peace, surrounded by a loving family.

LIFE AND ITS CEASELESS CHALLENGES

"Don't die with your music still inside you.
Listen to your intuitive inner voice and
find what passion stirs your soul."
- Wayne Dyer

Life is an ever-changing series of events. A sudden shift, and the strongest people sometimes lose their resilience and objectivity. They become depressed and negative, which diminishes the natural fighting spirit of the body. The immediate response can be fight or flight. Your mind chooses the path, and the body just follows.

Vipin, 75 years, had a successful career and was now enjoying a retired life. He resided in a large three-storey building with Nimrat, his wife, Mohanish and Ashish, his two sons, daughters-in-law and grandchildren. Each family occupied one floor. They led a comfortable, upper-class life. Vipin had a profitable run in his construction business and retired soon after an economic debacle in 2007-2008, when he lost so much money that he decided to wind up the business.

He had a land bank but, after weighing the pros and the cons, the family decided to keep away from the construction business as once again, they would have had to face private lenders, banks and irate investors on a regular basis. It was a tough business. Once burned, twice shy. There was no financial distress, even without the business, and the family settled down to a quiet, peaceful life without disturbing their upper-class standard of living. The sons dabbled in stock trading and money lending and kept themselves occupied and productive.

Whatever they did was with minimum risk, and the business was managed conservatively. Rahul, Rakul, Yuvraj and Yogita, the grandchildren, were well-educated and went to foreign universities for postgraduate studies. There was nothing much to complain about. God had indeed been kind. Vipin and Nimrat had the respect of the clan, and that mattered.

Vipin was an active, sporty kind of person with a large circle of friends and business associates. He and Nimrat would often embark on short pilgrimages; they were pious and ritualistic, and believed in a God who watched over them. But having tasted business success, the family couldn't remain quiet for too long. The temptation to make more money loomed over them and they plunged into the next construction boom in 2012. They had a land bank and so decided to put it to good use. Guarding free plots from encroachment was anyway a nightmare.

Once it was decided to dive into the construction business again, Vipin was roped in by the sons to head the operations. He was more than willing. He was healthy, full of energy and had the experience. But Nimrat was dead against this. "It took me three months to convince her," pointed out Vipin. "She kept saying that by the grace of *Wahe Guru* we have everything. He has been more than kind to us. Look at our lives, we have it all. Now it is time for us to serve people and use whatever time is left in spiritual activity. Contentment and *Hari bhajan* should guide us and not greed or commercial activity. But I was of the opinion that if my sons needed my experience in setting up the business, it was my duty to help them. I could retire once the business was on track. I would even joke that I was fortunate to get a second innings and a chance to retire twice."

After initially resisting the idea vehemently, Nimrat finally conceded. "She saw that my heart was in the business and I would be very unhappy if I didn't help my sons," continued Vipin. "I convinced myself that once the teething problems were taken care of, I would retire. Somewhere, at the back of my mind, I also wanted to prove myself, as I had to shut down my business quite abruptly earlier. I didn't want to be a failure in life."

Nimrat understood this but had seen so much upheaval in their lives in the past due to the business, that she was afraid of a replay. "She told me quite emphatically that any stress at this age would impact us very badly, however fit we may be," added Vipin. "She had stood by me like a rock all these years. It was her continuous emotional support that kept me going and bailed me out of various unsavoury situations. I understand now, in hindsight, that she had a sixth sense."

Vipin restarted the business in 2013. "It took us some time to get permissions and start the construction," he explained. "Just before Diwali 2014, we launched one of our projects and started construction. Things started to move, although not at the speed we wanted."

The office was close to home and Nimrat would sometimes drop by with lunch and the whole family would sit together for a meal. "It started to feel like old times as I was spending a lot of time in the office. Even Nimrat started to relax. Business was steady and more streamlined than the first time around. We had learned our lessons and promised never to repeat them."

Vipin was determined to succeed this time.

And then came the shock. Demonetisation was announced in 2016. All cash in circulation came to a halt and most businesses stalled. It was a sudden move to flush out black money from the economy. There was mayhem and confusion. No one knew what would happen in the days to come. Businesses came to a standstill. Even depositing or withdrawing money from accounts became difficult.

"We were at crossroads as we had started our business just two years back, and had invested a lot of our own capital, as it was not easy to get loans. We borrowed a little from banks, managed the rest ourselves and sold some inventory," explained a distraught Vipin.

"We were all shocked by the turn of events but Nimrat was hugely affected as she had sensed that something bad would happen. We were trying to act brave but we knew that it would be an uphill task for small builders like us. It would be impossible to sell further inventory until we finished the projects on hand. Given the resources at our disposal it was going to be quite difficult.

"I was worried about Nimrat and even guilty of pushing her into this mess when we had a comfortable life going, especially after she had warned me. Nimrat kept a brave front but her discomfort was visible to me. She tried to follow her routine and kept going for her evening walks and temple visits. But, under it all, she was suffering."

One evening Nimrat had a fall in the park, where she had gone for a walk with her group of friends. She had acute pain in the back and was unable to stand up. An X-ray confirmed that she had suffered a compression fracture of the spine. At 70, surgery was not a good idea.

The doctors explained that the process of recovery would require at least three months of bed rest. In addition to rest, Nimrat was prescribed painkillers and massage therapy. She had to use a back brace, which would limit her movements, but take the pressure off her painful bones. However, to prevent bone atrophy, she was advised to move around.

Depending on her recovery, a rehabilitation program to strengthen her back could be started. The doctors assured the family that complete recovery was possible with Nimrat's cooperation.

But the family business was in a mess and Nimrat was in a great deal of stress even thinking about it. Her fall was the start of an emotional downhill run.

By November 2017, two weeks after the fracture, it was apparent that Nimrat was giving up the fight. Her elder daughter-in-law contacted one of our counsellors and we were promptly engaged by the family to assess the situation and provide emotional support. Nimrat's history revealed the deep trauma that she had suffered from the collapse of the first innings of the business. She had stood by her husband through thick and thin but was feeling slighted by his insistence on re-starting the business and not listening to her gut instinct.

"I feel humiliated when he does not respect my judgement," she divulged. "Even earlier, I was always supportive of him and ended up submitting to his decision. When we are partners, the least he can do is pay heed to what I say. We have gone through so much and emerged out of all the troubles by the grace of Wahe Guru. He acknowledges that it would not have been possible without me by his side. But when it comes to decision making, he has the last word. It has always been like that. What about the trauma that I have gone through due to his unilateral decisions?"

At *HalloHappiness* we could clearly see that Nimrat's anxiety was converting into depression and, if not addressed immediately, could turn very serious; she would not be able to come out of her trauma unscathed.

We worked on her emotional state, which was fast deteriorating. Nimrat was feeling devalued by the man she deeply loved and had submitted to. She accepted his love and unflinching commitment to her, but deep down felt that he didn't respect her opinions.

Nimrat was also frightened of the future. What would happen to her children and grandchildren if the family finances crumbled? How would they find life partners of similar status, and how would they be able to live on a tight budget after a lifetime of comfortable living? A series of doubts assailed her troubled soul.

We worked first on stabilising Nimrat's emotions and then enhancing her desire for life with positive affirmations. She was always happy to talk about her past and about how the family had overcome obstacles together. In the initial years, when the boys were little, she had single-handedly shouldered the responsibility of bringing them up, and had done a wonderful job. These became trigger points in shifting her emotions into a positive frame.

Her resilience started to grow, and so did her recovery. Gradually, she started to acknowledge that a positive outcome was possible, with determination and hard work. Now that there were three people working things out, not just her husband, she became confident that the situation would improve.

By the fourth week, slowly and steadily, she started showing signs of improvement. Instead of being in bed most of the time she started engaging in life. She also realised that Vipin had no intention to deliberately humiliate her as he truly respected her. If he had pained her in any way, it was purely unintentional. "Everything started to happen for me after Nimrat came into my life," affirmed Vipin, heaping praise on his wife. He fervently believed that it was just a passing phase and it would all come together if Nimrat supported him now.

Nothing would last forever.

Nimrat is happy and content once again. With Vipin by her side, she has recovered completely and is now actively involved in the day-to-day life of her family. "Once again, by the grace of Wahe Guru, all is well." Her belief in life and the Almighty has been restored.

Learnings:

1. We believe that the important 20 per cent initial recovery, in any prolonged illness, starts with emotional health. It supplements physical recovery and enhances the process, reducing the time taken for complete rehabilitation.

2. It is vital to acknowledge the partner in close relationships. And, more importantly, to communicate it.

3. In our fast-paced lives, these small gestures up the value quotient in relationships.

4. Women have become more participative in every aspect of life. In fact, they run the households and play lead roles in family businesses. They need to be acknowledged.

5. Gargantuan male egos are misplaced in such situations as women have become more than equal partners. As we see all around us, women have excelled in all spheres.

MARRIAGE: LOVE'S LABOUR LOST?

BROKEN HEARTS, BROKEN HOMES

"One of the most courageous decisions you'll ever make is to finally let go of what is hurting your heart and soul."
- Brigitte Nicole

Although she did not tell us the name of her hometown, we guessed it was some picturesque hilly area of India. The descriptions of the hills, the long rows of cedar trees, the scent of the muddy earth and the narrow *pagdandi* leading to her school, were vivid.

"It would take an hour's walk to school on normal days, and maybe two hours on a rainy day," explained Radha. She was never too sure of the time taken for anything since there was no timepiece around. They lived by cosmic time, by the diktats of the seasons, and school would never punish them if they were late. So, time was never a concept to be feared or even accounted for. "I never thought about time. Like all aspiring singers, I walked the distance, singing Bollywood numbers I had heard on the radio. I secretly hoped that one day I too would be acclaimed for my voice."

Attending school was a welcome change from the domestic drudgery. There were now a handful of girl students in class, as literacy for girl children was being vigorously promoted in the slow, sleepy villages of Kumaon, in Uttarakhand. Bound on the north by Tibet, on the east by Nepal, on the south by Uttar Pradesh and on the west by the Garhwal region, Kumaon was nestled safely in a time warp, cuddled in a Himalayan embrace.

Hailing from a financially sound background, Radha had an edge as her father, being the eldest in the family, commanded respect; it was the norm in a rural community. He was looked up to and his word was law.

Jobs were seasonal and incomes scarce. In material terms, the village didn't have much to boast of. But they lived in the lap of the mountains, in picturesque surroundings, and material wants were few. The land provided them most of what they needed. There were about 30 houses, and 15 children attended school, of whom three were girls, who were granted special privileges.

Radha was a fairly good student and dreamt of becoming a doctor. But those dreams were shattered when her father died when she was barely out of school. A family feud ensued over the property, the other male members of the family usurped their land, and she and her mother, Bhavani, were thrown out of their home. The extended family thought it was not profitable to feed a widow, and were wary of a girl child who could, one day, assert her rights over the property, thanks to the rules of a matriarchal society.

So, a young girl, barely 17, and her young mother, packed their bags and landed in New Delhi, at the home of a distant relative. But there was more domestic discord, and they had to leave in a hurry. A young widow and her nubile daughter would draw uninvited attention, they were told.

Radha and her mother arrived in Mumbai, the City of Dreams. It was a far cry from the comfortable and familiar confines of Kumaon. Terrifying at first, but also dazzling, a fantasyland she had never conjured of, Mumbai would now be her city to dream big.

If you are prepared to work hard, Mumbai rarely lets you down. It is India's economic hub and dream factory that embraces every immigrant without judgement. If you have it in you, the impossible can be achieved. For the overtly ambitious and unscrupulous, even the stars are within reach. If nothing else, there are crumbs and leftovers. But no one goes hungry.

Bhavani, her mother, soon started getting roles as an extra in Bollywood films thanks to her fair complexion, svelte, lithe frame and pretty looks. Radha would accompany her to the sets. These cameo roles provided enough to survive in a new city, without being dependent on some friendly relative. Soon, Radha's singing talent was discovered and she started getting offers to sing in a chorus. However, the money was not enough to fund her dream of a medical career, so Radha opted for a graduation in commerce.

After her graduation, Radha got a job in a corporate office at the junior-most level. It is here that she met Subir and fell in love.

Subir had lost his parents in a recent accident and had a sister who was married. Both, he and Radha, were going through a challenging phase in their lives, found common ground emotionally, and fell in love.

After a brief courtship, they decided to get married. Subir didn't object to Bhavani living with them. He had a two-bedroom apartment which accorded them their privacy. Radha quit her job to manage the household. She was finally enjoying domestic bliss after a long period of trials and tribulations. For the first time since leaving her home in the hills, she was happy. For the first time, there was peace.

Then things happened in quick succession. First, she lost her mother, her biggest strength. Then her sister-in-law's husband passed away, and in the midst of it all, Radha delivered a beautiful, healthy, baby girl. The birth of Aishwarya was a joyous and welcome relief and somehow provided closure to the loss of her mother.

But life is never a bed of roses. Despite the joy of her baby's birth, Radha was pensive. "God doesn't like my being happy for a long time. My mother was just seeing good days after so much struggle in her life, when He took her away. I really miss her and regret that she couldn't see Aishwarya, a name she had suggested for my daughter."

As life began to settle down, after all the upheaval, Subir brought Sukanya, his sister, back from her in-law's house, as they were ill-treating her. Once again, a widow had become a burden.

Sukanya needed a change of scene to sort out her emotional issues. She also needed a place to live. Her anxiety led to frequent emotional outbursts. Since Radha had seen her mother face a similar situation, she could empathise with her.

As days passed into months and there was no sign of Sukanya returning to her in-law's place, it became evident that she was planning to stay with them permanently. Radha's initial generosity started to diminish as she realised the enormity of the situation. When asked about his sister, Subir's nonchalant response was, "She will go when she decides. Leave it to her." He refused to take a stand on the issue.

Radha's questions met with a stone wall. She was on the brink of a nervous breakdown. It was difficult to cope with Sukanya's caprices and outbursts. Weighing all her options, she decided to take up a job to escape the emotional drama at home.

Aishwarya was left at a crèche, much against Subir's wishes. "It was not the best arrangement," admitted Radha. "If my mother was alive I would have happily left Aishwarya with her, but Sukanya was another story. I would never leave my child with her. She could even harm Aishwarya. I didn't trust her."

The new job brought her much-needed money and some stability, but happiness still eluded her. She missed spending time with her daughter, who was growing up alone; the daughter too missed the comforting presence of a mother. Radha's emotional life suffered and, by her own admission, intimacy with her husband had also died. Over time, Subir had decided not to acknowledge her presence.

The marriage was crumbling. She was forced into submission on important issues and couldn't take any decisions on her own. "Maybe he knew I had nowhere to go and took advantage. Or maybe he didn't want a confrontation, as he couldn't ask his sister to leave," Radha conjectured.

As the days passed, Sukanya's behaviour worsened and showdowns were frequent. "Her own frustrations were taking an emotional toll on all our lives. After so many years of living hell, I still had no clue how the situation would sort itself out," lamented Radha. "I tried to cajole her to take up some work, but whatever Sukanya embarked upon ended in fights and financial losses. Aishwarya had an unstable home and that tormented her. She was growing up and needed her space. She became defiant and would taunt me with over-smart replies. I often wondered if all this would affect her later on in life, as it had affected me. I would often think of my childhood in the mountains. We had no fancy trappings but were content and emotionally rich."

And then, COVID-19 descended on their already tumultuous lives, followed by the lockdown and a new script...

Radha's story unfolded gradually over a number of calls. It was as though she was reliving a dream sequence or, in this case, the nightmare that had taken over her entire existence.

Sometimes people take a long time to make a minor decision, and often take a major decision in haste.

From the innumerable calls we started receiving, we realised that there was a sudden urgency among people to decide on a definite course of action. Suddenly, failings and mortality seemed to be staring people in the eye. Closeted in their homes, without the usual social contact, and no sense of the future, imaginary fears, apprehensions and complexities were tormenting them. Depression and other psychological issues were rampant.

Radha explained her life story in detail as she wanted an unbiased perspective. She was looking for validation. So much had gone wrong in her young life that she didn't want to make any more wrong choices.

She had realised that the current scenario with Subir wouldn't last long. Life at home had ceased to be fun; in fact, it had become torturous. "It was clear to everyone but Subir," pointed out Radha. "How could he be so blind to what was going on?"

To her credit, she had invested in a small house for herself in the hills back home, a secret she had shared only with Aishwarya. Even Subir wasn't privy to it. Now, she had made up her mind to return to her roots. "I don't want to die a sad death," she confessed. "Apart from Subir, nobody knows the real struggle of my life and the emotional trauma I have lived through. With my savings, I can lead a comfortable life back home and shift my daughter to a hostel, as she has secured admission to a medical college. It might be my destiny to live alone in my later years as I don't want to be a burden on my daughter when she decides to get married."

In my capacity as a counsellor, I reasoned with her to weigh all the options, as this would be an irreversible decision. She agreed that

Subir would not be able to manage without her but argued, "How long can I live with a man who can't take a stand for his wife and child when he sees them suffering? He is also suffering, but it is better for one life to suffer than three."

She did promise to settle for a trial separation and spend some time in the hills to think things over. But she was also quite certain that there was no going back to Subir. The marriage, it seemed, had ended irrevocably. Or maybe not, because sometimes when we spend time in isolation by ourselves, we ponder a lot internally. It could work both ways, as nobody can predict the turning point when it comes to unpredictable human emotions.

Learnings:

1. Marital harmony needs hard work. There is no hard and fast rule for a successful marriage as each situation is unique.

2. In my experience as a counsellor, I have seen too many 'happy endings' sabotaged by loneliness. Loneliness binds people together and so the outcome of a separation will depend on how the individuals can cope with loneliness. We often set out on a course of action not anticipating the outcome. It is always possible for Radha and Subir to reconcile after a short separation once they address their individual loneliness living away from each other.

3. Dream sequences are just that – dreams. Reality has a way of worming in and hijacking all plans. What may seem rosy in our dream sequence can be very different in real life.

4. Sometimes simple dynamics create complex situations, they can break families. Sometimes near and dear ones may land up in irreconcilable differences.

5. Mumbai, once again, lived up to its reputation as the City of Dreams. Once again, the lives of a young mother and her daughter, cast away from home, were resurrected by the welcoming embrace of this melting pot. How many more runaways can this city hold to its bosom?

HOMEMAKER OR HOMEBREAKER: THE BIG DILEMMA OF COVID-19

"Don't let a little dispute injure a great relationship."
- *Tenzin Gyatso, the 14th Dalai Lama*

In his first call to *HalloHappiness*, Sunny confessed that he used to be a sunny guy, and so was named 'Sunny' by his parents. Family and friends applauded the decision. He belonged to a large family. Sunny's father had eight brothers and sisters and his mother had five sisters. Add children and grandchildren and extended family to the lot and it made a small village!

Fair, good-looking, joyous and extremely active, Sunny was just that – always sunny! But everything changed suddenly with

COVID-19 and its life-changing effect on all of humanity. When asked what had caused his disposition to alter so dramatically, he responded, "Just a month of Work From Home (WFH) has changed everything. I am not sunny anymore, just forlorn."

In their thirties, Sunny and his wife Rashmi, were a working couple. While he was employed in a private bank and worked erratic hours, she was in a government job with relatively fixed timings and greater job security. Apart from his extremely demanding work schedule, Sunny also had to keep tabs on the official launches and dinner engagements of his organisation.

Rashmi was also well-qualified to take up a demanding, highly-paid private sector job, but they had agreed that one partner would be the breadwinner and the other would provide the butter on the toast. Rashmi had no complaints with this arrangement as she felt very strongly about the woman being at home to look after and nurture the family. A ten-to-five job gave her all that. She had financial independence and domestic bliss, living life at her own comfortable, unhurried pace.

Both of them belonged to established families of Bhopal. Sunny was a handsome, smart, charming and popular lad. Rashmi was attractive and well-educated. They lived close by, came from the same socio-economic class and had common friends. It is customary for people in India to recommend eligible brides and grooms to each other. One thing led to another. The two met, their families met and their marriage was arranged. Both came from liberal backgrounds, so they could meet often and developed a fondness for one another prior to the nuptials. Before starting a family, they decided to travel the world and get to know one another really well.

"Those were the great adventure years of our lives," exulted Rashmi and Sunny in unison. "We loved every minute." They settled down to domesticity, saved money, went the regular route of having children, made smart investments and bought a plush two-bedroom apartment with a bank loan. They had planned it all out; to live well and save for a comfortable life and future. Everything seemed to be in place.

But man proposes and God disposes...

Life changed overnight for them with COVID-19 and the lockdown. They realised that if the economic blockade continued for over six months, their jobs would be in jeopardy. More importantly, with no friends and other activities to engage them, their relationship was being hauled over the coals. There were no distractions and spending so much time with each other, under one roof, started taking its toll.

The lockdown was a savage mirror into their lives as a couple. "I realised the mistakes we made in our assessment of each other, but never imagined the differences to be so wide," confessed Sunny. "We had completely missed noticing the apparent diversity in our basic personalities."

He continued in angst. "The banged doors, the un-uttered words and walk-outs are all pent-up, unexpressed emotions. This period of uncertainty is a reality check and is deeply impacting our lives, emotions and relationship. It is now also taking a toll on our health."

Sunny sounded distraught, "Even normal conversations end up in accusation flinging. Nothing seems to matter now, not even my own life. We are stuck in a situation with no way out. The future is uncertain, we could be in debt if the economic slowdown continues, and we have nothing in common for the relationship to flourish. Forget about the relationship flourishing or being on an even keel; it is a complete disaster."

Rashmi admitted that she was equally disappointed by all the expectations from her. "Sunny starts work at nine in the morning and finishes around ten at night. He expects me to be the super woman and accomplish everything like clockwork. I am also in WFH mode, which he is aware of. Both the children are given homework which I am supposed to complete for them. The children are also restless and want to get out and play, but it is my responsibility to handle them. As the lady of the house, it is my responsibility to see that everything runs smoothly. In short, everything is my responsibility. But saddled with my own office work and no resources in the form of maids, it is humanly impossible to work round the clock."

Rashmi had to oversee the children's education, their food requirements, their online classes and homework, their tantrums and silly fights, Sunny's demands, the household cleaning, in addition to her own office work. "It's not just the cuppa tea and the 'me time' I miss, but I feel like a stranger in my own home. I feel like a utility item. I wish Sunny could see and acknowledge that I am becoming bitter with my life in general, and specifically with him. This situation has become overwhelming. The entire burden is on me and no one understands what I am going through. Sunny is constantly under pressure from his office. But the least he can do is be thankful for what I am doing and demonstrate that in some form. He is not the only one tired at the end of the day. I am also human and can only do so much. I can also get tired."

Breakups are never a simple solution and Sunny and Rashmi also understood this as a mature couple. With our mediation both could sit together and decide on the best route for their future, as the pandemic was a temporary situation. Their children provided the emotional bond in the relationship.

While women are feeling overextended by juggling office and home responsibilities, most consider it their duty to take care of the household. Whether this stems from the belief passed on by the older generation, or a natural sense of sacrifice, a virtue specific to women, is debatable. But, undoubtedly, women are feeling trapped in outdated beliefs and role expectations.

Unfortunately, life in the big cities, with all the trappings, does not allow enough time for real emotional connect between partners, especially if they are both working. Face to face now, 24x7, without any distractions barring a blaring television set, all that they see in each other are the warts and moles. Familiarity does indeed breed contempt.

It may be premature to assess the real emotional impact of this global pandemic at this point in time. But it will be interesting to document how both genders, under varying socio-economic situations, in different parts of the world, have handled it. The emotional toll could well be greater than the physical one.

Learnings:

1. Women are feeling overstretched. Multi-tasking and unreasonable demands on them have taken their toll.

2. They definitely feel unappreciated for all the efforts they make to please every member of the family.

3. A little emotional support or appreciation would go a long way towards restoring their emotional balance and happiness, as they are natural givers.

4. Conversation and dialogue, with a dash of patience, even from one partner, can resolve issues for a better tomorrow. Start dialogue, listen patiently, make conversation.

PARADISE LOST

———

"My most brilliant achievement was my ability to be able to
persuade my wife to marry me."
- Winston Churchill

People from all walks of life head to Mumbai in search of a better quality of life, better job opportunities and that elusive pot of gold.

The pressures are tremendous. Some make it. Others get swallowed in the ebb and flow of the megalopolis. Those who fail, find it difficult to come to terms with their situation. It is an ego blow. Unable to accept reality and re-start life on another track, they are diffident and unwilling to return home. Failure is not easy to accept, yet hope of a more promising tomorrow, and the temptations of a big city, keep them rooted.

Terms like 'back home' and 'native place' creep in to establish the mental distance from home and a sense of belonging to the big city. It's a new persona in a new life.

Ravi was a freelance portrait painter and sculptor. He completed a course in fine arts from a college in U.P. and moved to Mumbai in search of better prospects. He looked around for jobs, couldn't settle in any one slot and decided to freelance, as it suited his temperament.

As a freelancer, there is no steady stream of income, payments are irregular and the competition severe. It demands hard work, talent, perseverance and luck than a full-time job. Most freelancers eventually look for other ways to supplement their income.

"I enjoy my freedom, thanks to the bonus of workhour flexibility," declared Ravi happily, oblivious to the risks. Robust and good-looking, he carried himself with an air of authority. He bumped into his neighbour, Revathi – dusky, petite, attractive, with cascading black hair – and was smitten. A short courtship later, they tied the knot.

Both their families weren't in favour of the union. Mr. Rajan, Revathi's father, used to see Ravi hanging around the building compound and wasn't impressed with his casual approach to life and work. He assumed that Ravi was unemployed, living off his parents. But since young lovers brook no opposition, the marriage was agreed upon.

Mr. Rajan had retired as a senior officer in the upper echelons of the corporate world. He had lived well and had brought up Revathi in the lap of luxury. She was well-educated, widely travelled and after marriage, took up a middle management corporate job.

Revathi started working a few years into the marriage as she realised that Ravi's uncertain income wouldn't help provide for the family. They now had two growing children, Samay, 6 years, and Sara,

5 years. So far, the couple had proved their parents wrong. Life was comfortable, they were content and that was what mattered.

But how long could the fairytale last? Enter COVID-19 and the lockdown and the script changed.

Ravi sounded vulnerable when he called. "You see, I am a bit of a free soul. I have never enjoyed being bound to timings in a proper job but COVID-19 has changed my perspective completely. I would gladly trade this situation for a proper, paid job, however mundane. It would probably be more interesting than looking after my kids full-time and assisting in the kitchen part-time. All this was novel for a few days but not fun anymore."

The home quarantine and constant domestic demands were getting unbearable. He added, "This life seems so strange that sometimes I wonder if, a few months ago, I was living some other incarnation. Am I supposed to feel like this at 35? I really feel lost and wonder if life will ever be normal again. Being an artist and an emotional person, I am unable to take the pressure. Why do you think life is being so unfair to me? These restrictions are taking a toll and I often feel very fearful. Sometimes I am filled with negative thoughts and I have even been thinking of taking my life."

Revathi was feeling even more pressure. Being the provider for the last few years, she was unable to foresee a normal future for the family. Her anxiety levels were sky high as she feared she might get laid off or be forced to accept a salary cut. Her fears were real. With the economic slowdown, people were getting laid off everywhere.

With no upturn in the economy in sight, the long Work From Home (WFH) hours had taken a toll on her emotional health. Having had a stable income and comfortable life all along, her fears were genuine.

"My father will never forgive me," she said. "If we are unable to afford our children's education and provide them a comfortable life, he will be relentless. He has always compared my marriage to my sister's, who is well-settled with a groom of my father's choice."

The lockdown was making Ravi feel trapped and disillusioned. "This is taking a toll on our personal lives too, even our intimacy," he confessed. "Revathi is often complaining of my carefree lifestyle and lack of savings. With two little kids to bring up, the situation is bleak. We end up fighting and saying nasty things to each other. Life is under so much stress now that it is totally devoid of any pleasure. For someone who eloped to marry me against her family's wishes, and has lived with me for 10 years, I expect support at this stage and not the blame game I am being subjected to. To make things worse, one can't even go out and meet friends or have them over. There is no escape."

We explained to them that these were trying times for everyone, as no one was mentally or emotionally equipped for a pandemic of this magnitude. The whole world was in a similar situation, with people trying to adapt to the new normal. With our intervention they took out some time to talk things out, which was a start to tamper their frayed nerves. Interaction with other couples facing similar situations also helped.

Uncertainties are real. The effects of the pandemic are just rolling out and a new synergy will develop once things settle down. Human resilience, the ability to reinvent and a positive outlook will help stabilise the quagmire of emotions.

Learnings:

1. Roles and responsibilities have changed during the pandemic. It has rocked the fundamentals of marriage and togetherness. Gone are the space and freedom of the past that allowed relationships to survive, and family members to coexist. With forced proximity and delegation of duties, frustrations are at a peak and confrontations ugly.

2. Communication, the biggest pillar of any relationship, is the only solution in these situations. Inter-dependence in close relationships is vital. It makes both persons feel wanted. If this gives way, the relationship is on the rocks.

3. The COVID-19 lockdown bore witness to many relationships breaking down. Marriages were on the verge of collapse. Family bonding was tested and, in many cases, just gave way. With no appreciation and support, partners felt forced to introspect and make tough choices.

4. Every change calls for re-adjustment when the delicate balance is disturbed. The COVID-19 pandemic called for unusual effort to sustain relationships.

5. It helps to remember that nobody had experienced something as unpredictable as COVID-19 and everybody was struggling, in their own space, to deal with it as best they could. Suicides,

pregnancies, break-ups and a variety of emotional and physical illnesses added to the COVID-19 lockdown anecdotes. Caregivers, both emotional and physical, had their tasks cut out.

ISOLATION PANGS

"Let there be spaces in your togetherness. And let the winds
of the heavens dance between you. Love one another but
make not a bond of love; Let it be rather a moving sea
between the shores of your souls."
- Kahlil Gibran, The Prophet

Arjun was a regular caller for several months. He enjoyed talking to
us at *HalloHappiness.*

He was not a typical Mumbai boy as a good part of his childhood
was spent travelling with his father. Being an only child, he was
pampered. In his words, "I had the opportunity to explore a lot
of things on my own. My father's transferable job gave me ample
reason to grow beyond my years. I saw and learnt a lot from my
continuously changing surroundings, as I was an observant child."

After his father retired, the family settled down in Mumbai. Arjun's
regular, peppy calls to us helped vent his feelings of the day, most of
which was spent in the office. This was his second job in the private
sector. He was now in a much bigger organisation, with increased

salary, perks and responsibilities. It was a promotion, a substantial jump. The only disadvantage was more pressure and less time for the family.

Anita, his wife of five years, was a homemaker. Cultured and educated, she busied herself with their two-year-old son, managed the staff and kept her parents-in-law company. It was a tranquil, stereotypical, household. "Being the only son, it was natural for my parents to live with me," said Arjun. "Thankfully, my wife is happy with this arrangement."

He would call us at *HalloHappiness* at 7.45 pm every day, speak for an hour and sign off promptly at 8.45 pm with a breezy, "Talk to you tomorrow guys, same time. I have offloaded myself of office politics and will have a peaceful time at home with wife and family. Don't need to bother them with all this."

The conversation included simple, day-to-day office banter, marinated with a little spicy gossip and sometimes even hilarious titbits. He needed to offload office anxiety and we lent him a patient ear. He enjoyed it and we loved listening to him.

Then, of course, COVID-19 happened and everything changed.

There were no calls from Arjun for a month. Then, one day, he called unexpectedly. He sounded serious and subdued. The focus of the conversation had shifted from the office to the home front. His cheerful, talkative persona had given way to a melancholic, dejected, lifeless one.

"I thought life was tough in the office," he started off. "But now it seems like a piece of cake. I thought I used to be stressed and that's why I called you to lighten the load. But I never imagined spending time in WFH (Work From Home) mode could make me so stressed. Working with 95 people in the office seems easy in comparison. I never felt claustrophobic or emotionally stretched. There are only five members at home but the demands are huge. Being an ideal son, husband and father seems like a Herculean task. Not that I mind the demands, as I have always been the responsible type. But it just seems that nobody loves me for the person I am. It is all about being the provider."

Arjun seemed desperate. He hadn't spoken to us for a long time and seemed to be making up for the absence with a vengeance. He rattled on. "My wife, who never expected me to do any household chores earlier, now complains that I do nothing at home. But I believe that I am contributing more than ever. Earlier, I was in the office and nothing was expected of me.

"My wife and I are feeling unwanted, neglected and unappreciated. There never seems to be a good time to say the right things to each other. I feel disconnected from her, both physically and mentally, and sometimes wonder if we will ever be able to go back to a normal married life after the lockdown is over. Some equations have changed 360 degrees and I am finding it difficult to recognise the person that she once was. I guess she is feeling the same."

Arjun's anguish was intense. "When I used to go to office and spend less time at home, I looked forward to some private time with my wife over a cup of tea and biscuits on my return from work. On some days I would even spend quality time with my parents, and my son would be happy to sit on my lap and play or watch cartoons on TV. Now, living within these closed walls for so long, all that doesn't seem to be a priority any more. We are seeing each other the whole day and there is no surprise element on either side.

"Additionally, I do feel guilty when I have to send my son away while I am working. His sad face haunts me. He thinks that since I am at home, I am available to indulge him. Of course, he is too small to understand the situation. Then he goes crying to Anita, who gets upset, as do my parents. At office I could work without disturbance in my cabin. This is not even a remote possibility now. Everyone thinks that because I am home, I am available for various chores, which is certainly not the case, as the workload has increased."

For Arjun, it was most frustrating to work from home, combined with the uncertainty of the future and the emotional distancing. "My life is limited to the bed, sofa and dining table," he complained. "There are too many disturbances and demands and I cannot function properly. Somehow, working from office provided a normalcy to life. There were clear demarcations: office, home and then some outdoor life. Now, everything has blurred and merged into one and it has become suffocating."

Arjun missed meeting with his colleagues and friends. He missed the gossip, the calls, the pranks, even the office politics, with its plotting and machinations. A gregarious and outgoing person, with a promising career ahead, he now felt isolated and lost. "I have no 'me' time," he complained. "Though I love my family, I need a break, to get out and meet new people. Besides, there is no privacy at all."

The Work From Home (WFH) shift due to the pandemic created new challenges. Earlier, housewives had some time to themselves at home and the men had an emotional buffer with friends and colleagues in the office and outside. Now, there was no escape or respite. Familiarity bred contempt. Tough marriages and relationships that survived on thin margins, because both partners saw little of each other on a normal working day, were irrevocably broken. Others were just about managing, trying to cope and make things work. Possibly, only young lovers and couples enjoyed the forced isolation.

We are used to a life that is dotted with several associations and activities. Besides home and office, we engage in extra-curricular activities and interact with people from various walks of life. The hobbies and classes we attend all add colour and variety to our day. There are travel plans, weekend getaways, movies, restaurants, clubs, shopping, a wide gamut of activities that keep us busy and entertained. When all this is taken away, there is nothing to look forward to.

In big cities like Mumbai, with space at a premium, entire families are holed into a one-bedroom unit. Like jailbirds, there is no escape. Mandatory masks and social distancing have sabotaged the fun element leading to depression and other psychological issues.

Every space is experiencing a shift. The work environment and culture has changed, and may not be the same ever again. There are job losses and pay cuts. Marriages and relationships are breaking down. No one is sure of how long the pandemic will last. All this uncertainty is wreaking havoc in the family structure.

Learnings:

1. Close relationships in 24/7 situations can be unreasonably demanding. But the solution does not lie in blame games. Communication between partners is the key and should never be allowed to break down.

2. Marital harmony (bliss is a distant word now) requires hard work. Space, understanding, compassion and setting aside egos are crucial to make the alliance work and be successful.

3. Friendship is the cornerstone. Remain friends and work as companions or co-workers. That can help build bonds and strengthen the foundations. Ultimately, the goal of every relationship is long-term companionship.

4. Important too, to add that spice and variety to our relationships. Remember, it is a two-way street. Taking out time for each other, even if it means stealing a walk down the road, or on the terrace, or dressing up for each other; it is the little things that work wonders on lasting bonds.

5. Many families have found the lockdown a blessing. They have taken the time to get to know each other, entertain and have fun with each other. Even working together at home is fun. It shows respect and appreciation for the home-maker, who has been silently doing the chores 24/7. It also makes her feel it is not just her "duty".

6. For the male members, especially in a patriarchal society like ours, it has been a wake-up call. While some have risen and pitched in, putting their 'entitled' attitude aside, some are feeling the heat and finding themselves 'trapped'.

7. In the end it is companionship, understanding and love which make the journey worthwhile.

Of course, there is *HalloHappiness*!

SEGMENT THREE

INFIDELITY, VIOLENCE, RAPE

RESURRECTION AFTER A DEAD MARRIAGE

"Marriage has no guarantees. If that's what you're looking for,
go live with a car battery."
- Erma Bombeck

Leena, 40-years-old, had been married for 18 years. Pretty, fair and tall, she was a striking personality. Independent, educated, from a well-off middle-class background, she enjoyed calling the shots. The first time she called us, she was driving. In between tears, she confessed, "I have been carrying your number for the past few days but couldn't muster enough courage to call." She spoke softly and it was difficult to decipher what she was saying through the tears. My first thought was to instruct her to stop driving and park the car somewhere. It was dangerous to drive, cry and speak on the phone at the same time. I waited patiently till she could speak coherently.

"My husband has left me for a much younger girl. I have been such a failure in my life. But my immediate concern is my daughter and her future. She is 19-years-old and will have to carry this stigma to her altar and beyond," Leena wailed. "He just walked out one day saying 'I can't handle this anymore'. He didn't give me a chance to find out what had happened, discuss what went wrong and, maybe, make amends." This was what I gathered from the first conversation. "Not only did he not speak to me, he didn't even bother about Sweety, our daughter. What will be her reaction when she knows that her father is involved with a girl close to her age?"

Leena had guessed that Rohan, her husband, was clandestinely seeing someone else for a while, but didn't imagine it to be serious. "That's why he left in such haste. This way he wouldn't have to offer any explanation. What explanation can he offer? He is the guilty party." After she regained some composure, I asked her to go back home, never to drive by herself in such an emotional state again, and call us when she was calm.

In her second conversation, she was a little contrite and ashamed of her earlier outburst, but comfortable to talk about her failed marriage. "We have always lived in Mumbai, as Rohan was working for the Merchant Navy. Three years ago, he got a lucrative offer from a company in Bengaluru. After some deliberation, he decided to take up this job. As our daughter was growing up and would soon be of marriageable age, the extra money seemed an attractive proposition. Rohan shifted to Bengaluru, and since Sweety was in college, it seemed practical for both of us to stay back in Mumbai. Every second weekend Rohan would visit us. All three of us were happy with the arrangement.

"After about six months, his visits became irregular," she continued. "He explained that it was due to an overload of work. I didn't think much of it then, as sometimes he would travel to Mumbai for work on weekdays too. I had no idea of his double life. His behaviour changed a bit, but he would always visit with a lot of gifts for both of us, and we would dine out or spend quality time together. And then, suddenly, he just decided to leave."

Leena called us regularly. In her initial calls she was hopeful of Rohan getting fed up of his liaison and returning back remorsefully to her but as time passed by, her anger subsided and she started reconstructing her life together. Slowly, her confidence, resilience and self-esteem grew. In the six months she was with us, we made a great deal of progress. She also took up a job in the firm where she had worked prior to her marriage. This not only boosted her confidence and provided some money, but also kept her mind occupied and away from the pain in her personal life.

"I still get anxious about the future but then feel grateful for getting a job after such a long break from work," she confessed. We kept building her morale and encouraging her, which she admitted was "most soothing to her agitated nerves and filled her with confidence." I complimented her on having adjusted to the new life so well and leaving behind her baggage so quickly. Leena had recovered and recouped well. She just laughed off the compliments, adding "what choice do I have"? but she knew that she was on the right track.

And then COVID-19 and the lockdown happened.

Leena sounded devastated in her next call to us. The slowdown in the economy was taking a toll and job cuts were becoming fairly rampant. All her earlier uncertainties and anxieties were resurfacing, and I was worried that she may slip into the depression like before she had enrolled with us. But sometimes, dire situations bring out the best in us. As they say, *dar ke aage jeet hai*. And that's exactly what happened with Leena.

After the initial days of panic, she was assured by her boss that she wouldn't lose her job. She began WFH (work from home) which also helped handle her home situation. Since she had started working, her daughter had felt neglected, as Leena couldn't devote much time to her. Leena felt guilty. Now, with the assurance from her boss and renewed confidence, she could devote time to Sweety, practice yoga and pursue other interests, all while meeting her work deadlines.

After eight months of separation from her husband and three months into the lockdown, Leena was a different person. Her confident 'Hello' on the phone, positive outlook towards life and long-term plans for her daughter, reflected the courage she had shown after Rohan walked out of their lives. He had approached her a few times to offer financial assistance but she refused. With her newfound independence she reasoned, "Why should I go back the route I left behind?

Brave words indeed, from an empowered woman.

Learnings:

1. Self-esteem is a very important part of building your relationships, not only with others, but also with yourself.

2. Self-esteem should be nurtured from an early age to shape your personality and thought process. It's a continuous process.

3. Sometimes, adversity brings out the best in people. Often even the meek, protected and cowardly find incredible strength in the face of challenges.

4. In tough times, it is important to meet with positive people and find solutions to get out of the morass. Nothing is ever over. There is always a solution.

5. When life throws challenges at us, it is prudent to be patient. Knee-jerk reactions are best avoided. Friends, elders and counsellors can always lend a valuable ear. Wait for a while, let the waters settle and then take a rational decision.

PATI, PATNI AUR WOH!

"Nothing in life is to be feared. It is only to be understood."
- Marie Curie

It was a warm, sultry afternoon when we received her call for the first time. Shubha was direct, to the point and wanted to know about the services we provide. We gave her a detailed explanation about our online services for mental health, immunity assessment and guidance. All this is available once you sign up with *HalloHappiness* and choose your package. We asked her to make her choice.

Shubha was 72-years-old and had enjoyed good health most of her life. But around the time she called us, she had started feeling a little tired as she was emotionally stretched. Her request was simple: "Will you help me overcome this? I think my immunity is getting impacted. I don't like the feeling and I don't like being dependent." We assured her that we would do our best.

Despite the passage of time, Shubha was still graceful and elegant. Not very tall, she quipped, "I have a straight spine and so appear taller than my 5 feet 2 inches." She had two daughters, both in their fifties, one living in the USA and the other in Bengaluru. She missed them, of course, but never complained. Both the daughters visited her at least once a year and she was comfortable with the arrangement.

She lived well in a well-appointed, compact apartment in the suburbs of Mumbai. It was close to the sea and she admitted to being enchanted by the sound of lapping waves that she could hear from her living room window.

"My husband passed away suddenly in an accident, almost 20 years ago, and I went through a lot of trouble sorting out our financial affairs," she confided in one of our conversations. "That did take a toll on my health, as his sudden demise did not provide him the time to organise everything. Luckily, the apartment was in my name and I only had to worry about the other things. I had a roof over my head and that was important. Otherwise, it would have been impossible to live in Bombay all by myself." She added as an afterthought, "Don't mind me saying this but I can never think of my good old Bombay as Mumbai."

Shubha's husband was a fairly successful businessman and money was never a problem. They led an upper middle-class life. "I loved to drive earlier but now I keep a driver. So, I haven't driven for the past 15 years or so. Maybe I should try to do that one day to shock everyone," she chuckled, sharing titbits about her life, slowly opening the window to her soul.

Our conversations continued for weeks. One day, she didn't appear to be her usual chirpy self. She seemed visibly upset but just complained about life in general without being specific. We sensed that something was wrong but left it at that, not wanting to pressure her. If the matter was important, she would tell us in her own sweet time.

"How dare she come to my house to ask something from me?" was her opening salvo when she called next. We were baffled, taken by surprise. Who was she referring to? Who was this new person in her life?

In earlier conversations, she hadn't mentioned her husband's second marriage and how she had to fight legal battles to safeguard her interests and not allow the other woman "to steal" from her. This came as a surprise. We just joined the dots.

"Those were very stressful days and it took a heavy toll. But I made sure that she could not get away with much as she had no rights," Shubha continued about the other woman who had married her husband and was now the cause of her unrest.

"Since she has a son, I did leave her with something. I didn't want to see them on the streets. But I never forgave my husband for doing this to me. I also don't appreciate anyone defending him, and some have tried. He fooled me for many years and never told me the truth. It was a shock when I came to know all this only after his death. That woman just landed up at my house claiming things about my late husband. I had to be strong and tactful in throwing her out, as I didn't want any complications for me and my daughters."

Shubha's maid Piyu, in her 40s, was from a small village in Odisha. She had been with Shubha for over 15 years. Shubha was very generous to Piyu as somewhere she identified with common bond of their husbands being unfaithful to them and the struggle they had to face in their lives. Extremely vigilant and dedicated to her Kaki, she travelled to her hometown once every two years after alternative arrangements were made for her mistress. Strict instructions were laid out for Piyu to return on the scheduled date and not to delay her return even by a day. Since her railway ticket was booked by Shubha, the chances of her not arriving on time were dim. But the warnings were always issued and underscored.

Piyu was married and had a one-year-old son when she came to work for Shubha. Her husband of two years had disappeared one day, never to return. She hadn't heard from him for many years and had accepted the desertion. "Maybe it was for the best that I had to come down to Mumbai to explore other options and provide a better life to my son and mother in the village," she said. "My mother has been a real source of strength as she brought up my son, who is growing up well and studying hard. The least I can do is to take care of her in her old age."

Piyu was happy that with her earnings in Mumbai her family back home lived well. She enjoyed Shubha's confidence and had been her constant companion for many years. They shared a deep bond, having also seen the vicissitudes of life in their own ways.

"I can never leave her, whatever may happen in my life," she said quite emphatically and dramatically about Shubha. "She has been more than a mother to me. She taught me everything – cooking, cleaning, arranging things in the house. I was just a simple village girl."

Piyu was scheduled to travel to her village in January 2020 but the plans got delayed due to Shubha's health issues. The first time she fell ill, she recuperated at home. The second time necessitated hospitalisation. Once Shubha had fully recovered, Piyu was allowed to go to her village in Odisha, once again with the stern warning that she had to return on the stipulated date. She laughingly responded, "As though I have ever been delayed in all these years."

But who can alter divine plans?

When COVID-19 hit India and a lockdown was imposed, it was impossible for Piyu to return to Mumbai, what with travel restrictions and train services shutting down. Shubha grew impatient as the days passed. With no surety of Piyu's return, she hired a young maid. But, unable to tolerate Shubha's whims, the young girl simply disappeared one day.

Shubha was in a fix and started looking for alternative domestic help, which proved difficult given her irate behaviour. Due to the restrictions imposed by housing societies, part-time help was not an option, and Shubha, still waiting for Piyu, didn't want to hire a full-time person. Luckily, another couple in the building offered their full-time help to bail Shubha out until Piyu returned.

With every passing day, Shubha grew anxious and depressed as she waited for Piyu, who was now gone for over three months and not contactable. Her daughters were equally concerned and the elder daughter living in Bengaluru, promised to visit her mother as soon as the lockdown lifted and she could travel. With Piyu looking after their mother, the girls had grown comfortable, as it was impossible to drop everything to be with Shubha for long periods.

Piyu called after three months, but with distressing news. She explained that she couldn't return to Mumbai. Her Mumbai chapter was finally and irrevocably over. Her husband, who had disappeared for years, suddenly showed up and now wanted custody of their son. He had been living with another woman all these years. When he realised that his son had grown up and was educated, he thought he would be a good support for him in his old age. He used to visit him in Piyu's absence and had brainwashed him into going with him to Kolkata, the big city, with better jobs and higher pay.

Piyu's old mother couldn't prevent this, as they were never legally divorced. So the husband could walk in and out as he pleased.

Piyu was broken. "All my life I worked hard and educated my son, and now he is ready to go with his father," she protested. "I can see the male bonding and how he has brainwashed my son. I have no other choice but to stay behind and look after my mother, who is really old now. I also have to worry about my old age as I have no one to fall back on."

Similar circumstances in both their lives had bonded Shubha with Piyu. Both their men, in different ways, had been unfaithful to their wives. Shubha was materially better off, had a better support system and could overcome the challenges of old age and sickness with some adjustments. But Piyu's life in a small village in Odisha was inundated with challenges.

Learnings:

1. The pandemic left many of the elderly vulnerable, as they lacked an adequate support system. There was no sustainable structure for them to fall back on, particularly in nuclear, urban families. The problems in the rural setting, without money and jobs, were worse.

2. Migrant labour was stretched at all levels. There was very little support from the administration. With their survival at stake, migrant labourers, who formed the bulk of the support system network in the big cities, had to return to their hometowns, amidst extreme hardships.

3. Despite the government doing its best by providing rations and transport, people were far away from their families and burdened with the additional emotional stress of separation in a crisis.

4. India lives in its villages. We are essentially an agrarian society. The only way to stop or reduce the migration to urban centres is to develop the tier 2 and 3 towns and cities. Local industry will provide local employment.

5. Most important, a national policy will have to be formulated to assist senior citizens, who number a few hundred million. People need to be taken care of in their twilight years. That is the least a society can do.

LOVE, VIOLENCE AND DIVORCE

"Each time a woman stands up for herself without knowing it,
possibly without claiming it, she stands up for all women."
- Maya Angelou

I vividly remember the day Leena called. It was raining heavily, with thunder and lightning adding to the cacophony. Mumbai monsoons are at once breathtaking and intimidating!

Leena was hardly audible and I had to strain my ears to grasp what she was trying to say. One of the basic techniques in counselling is to allow a person to let go of their emotions and make space for unrestrained communication. I did the same in this case. I kept prodding her with sympathetic words, encouraging her to open up without fetters, all the while hoping that the rain would stop so I could hear her clearly.

"What is the use of being in love with a man like this?" She was talking about Neil, her husband of five years. "Whenever we go out, which is often, it ends the same way. He buys me the best clothes, takes me to expensive shows and treats me to expensive dinners, but then starts getting nasty as soon as he sees somebody looking at me admiringly. I don't consciously draw attention to myself. I dress up for him because I want to please him. If I am fair, tall and well-groomed, it is not my fault. I do stand out because of my height and I can't change my natural appearance, which is God given. Neil himself fell for my looks."

Leena continued unhindered. "He is also tall and carries himself well, but I don't feel insecure with the admiring glances he gets from other women. He is well-placed in the corporate world and is much sought after, but I don't create a scene. When we leave the house, he gives me admiring looks and praises me. But I feel that there are two people living in his head, and he can't decide which one should surface – when and where. When I don't dress up, he gets upset and says he likes me to be well-turned out, wants to be proud of his woman and for people to envy him. When I do dress well, he accuses me of tempting other men. So, which is the real Neil? Who is the Neil I am married to? How am I supposed to behave?"

Leena continued with a sigh, "When I look back at our courtship days, I remember he was very possessive, but never to this point of ugliness." She recalls an incident after a movie. "We were walking towards our car in the parking lot and I suddenly realised that Neil wasn't around. The next moment I saw him engaged in a brawl with a man who was parked a little distance away. After other people joined in and the matter was sorted out, I asked him what had happened. Instead of explaining the situation, he accused me of trying to attract the attention of the man he had to fight. This resulted in another fight between us which lasted days before he apologised." There were other incidents too; too many to be comfortable with.

"I am a good singer," she went on. "One evening, after a party in our house, a few friends hung around and we had an extempore singing session. One thing led to another and soon everybody joined in. It was fun. The night was long, we shared a lot of bonhomie, and by the time the last guests left, it was early morning.

"Then the situation got ugly. Short of hitting me, everything else was said and done. We had had a few drinks, and were a little high, but matters cannot get out of hand like this so often. We love each other, but his unpredictable behaviour upsets and demeans me."

Leena enjoyed Neil's possessive nature when they were dating in college. "While the other girls were neglected by their boyfriends, Neil would watch over me like a hawk and that made me feel loved and wanted. But I feel claustrophobic now after five years of marriage. I feel like calling it quits and walking out."

We suggested that Neil be brought online for counselling. We could hear his side of the story and he could, possibly, be shown another perspective. Leena tried, but couldn't persuade him. All along, her emotional state was getting frailer as she was never certain when the volcano would erupt again. "In his good mood, he can be caring and attentive, but at other times he is someone I don't know at all."

She kept calling us on and off for counselling. Her calls were triggered by some incident or the other, and she found solace in being able to share her fears with someone. Her mother lived alone in Mumbai, not very far from her. Her two married elder sisters resided in other cities. Her father had passed away recently, and Leena would occasionally visit her mother. It was during those visits that she would call us.

She called us again in March 2020 and cried. Neil had pushed her dangerously during an argument and there were suggestions of more physical violence. I opined that she should move out and maybe spend some time at her mother's place. She didn't want to drag her mother into this mess and had kept her domestic situation away from her till now. But this time she agreed with us and moved in with her mother for a few days.

Then came COVID-19, and the subsequent lockdown, which actually provided Leena a good excuse. She didn't have to explain much to her mother or to Neil about her extended stay. She called us and said, "God is on my side and is helping me sort this out." The days passed into weeks and Neil got the message. He realised that Leena wasn't keen on returning, even after the lockdown was relaxed. He kept calling her to convince her of his love, but Leena stood her ground and told him to get some professional help. "Otherwise I am not coming back," was her brave response.

Finally, after over a month of separation, Neil called us. "She doesn't understand me. I provide her with the best. She lives a comfortable life compared to her sisters, who move around in autos, while she has a car and driver." Neil said defensively, "I agree that I am a little short-tempered but I do look after her, and it is not that we are fighting every day. Occasionally, there is an incident, but, mind you, she is responsible for my behaviour." Is his conclusive statement.

We counselled Neil for over two months. This also worked well for Leena who got the time to think about her life and where she wanted to take it. She could sort out her emotions and look at Neil from a distance. Once Neil realised that she was serious about not coming back, his "macho" attitude started to shift. As a child, he had seen his uncle, who was the man of the house, hit his wife, and that had left an indelible impression on his psyche. He thought it was the macho thing to do.

Although Neil had hit her just once, the prolonged emotional abuse had taken its toll.

Domestic violence is a broad term and includes emotional abuse, intimidation by pushing, shoving, pulling the hair, kicking, using derogatory language, insults, criticism, humiliation, screaming and the like.

Learnings:

1. Look into the attacker's eyes and do not show fear.

2. Do not cry. It feeds the ego.

3. Raise your voice, say no to violence.

4. Work on your fears.

5. Violence is not being advocated here, but some knowledge of self-defence will help. If things get nasty, a woman should be equipped to protect herself.

6. Take the right route to solve your problems. There are many options available. Normally, when we refer to domestic violence, we assume that men are the perpetrators. But women are also to blame, and men also have avenues for redress. In fact, both partners have to be counselled.

In many surveys, over 40 per cent of women have been beaten by their husbands at some point in their lives. Over 51 per cent of men did not find anything wrong with it, and shockingly, 54 per cent of women thought it was justified. The good news is that the government has a lot of initiatives to empower women who are in the lower strata of society and who are not educated. They face the brunt of physical abuse. But there is no law against emotional abuse as it cannot be quantified, and encompasses a number of abstractions. There are initiatives too, for addressing the domestic violence men face, which may not be as physically daunting, but could be much more emotionally corroding.

MARITAL RAPE: AN ACT OF COWARDICE, NO OPTION FOR THE VICTIM

"I just want to sleep. A coma would be nice. Or amnesia. Anything just to get rid of this, these thoughts, whispers in my mind. Did he rape my head, too?"
- *Laurie Halse Anderson, Speak.*

Social media today is full of "happy couples" who, in truth, are living with a painful secret: lack of sexual intimacy. It's a paradox with which most women live their 'content and happy' lives. Relatively few talk about it and that's why we were surprised by Naina's call.

Naina, 45-years-old, lived with her husband Niteesh and their two children, 16-year-old daughter Deeksha and 14-year-old son Kshitij. She got married into a joint family that owned a joint business. The family split a few years after her marriage, and she moved into another house with her husband and children. For the last ten years she has run an independent household and by all yardsticks, enjoyed a successful marriage. Her husband proclaims to the whole world that she is his lucky charm as everything good happened in his life after Naina stepped in.

Naina approached us sometime in September 2020. She was candid about her problem of physical intimacy in her marriage. Like a lot of women, she lost interest in sex after her son was born. Niteesh was quite upset with the development and tried to reason with her. After a few years of persuasion, and Naina's unrelenting attitude, they reached a consensus. She allowed Niteesh to have sex outside of marriage.

It was an uncomfortable thought but she said, "I was so disinterested in any kind of intimacy, and disgusted with his persistence that this seemed the only solution." She opened up a little more and confessed to being a person of 'lower sex drive' from the beginning. "I never had much interest in sex while growing up, and all my friends used to make fun of me as I was never excited about reading the adult magazines popular in my college.

"I took physical intimacy as a 'necessary act' and lived with it in the initial years of marriage, but kept losing interest and felt repulsed every time Niteesh approached me. We were just not compatible, as I was no match for Niteesh's demands for physical intimacy. When we were in a joint family, the opportunity for intimacy was less as all the family members spent a lot of time together – at home, on vacations and even otherwise.

"We were living with twenty people in the joint family when Deeksha was born. Life was very hectic, and household chores kept all the women occupied, so my disinterest in intimacy was not noticed by Niteesh," she explained. "Once Kshitij was born, I was not just disinterested, but repulsed, by any physical intimacy. Niteesh was not happy as he wanted much more. This was becoming a sore point between us. Things started becoming ugly once we shifted to our new house and I had no choice but to allow him freedom." I was waiting for more, as I realised there was some untold portion.

She continued, "I haven't called you for a confession. It is my current situation which is causing me distress and I am unable to find a solution. Things were under control until the lockdown. Niteesh got desperate since he was not able to move out of the house to visit his regular spots for fulfilment of his sexual desires." Her voice was suddenly very low, almost inaudible. "For the last few months I am facing rape in my own house, by my own husband," she confided, and started to cry. She couldn't stop him from the act as he was her legally wedded husband.

She wanted to know if there was any way to protect herself under the circumstances, although she hoped that the end of lockdown would bring an end to her woes and life would go back to her 'normal'. For the sense of propriety, as she had two growing up children in the house, she was averse to take any step detrimental to their lives. The earlier arrangement had worked well for them in the past, as her children thought of them as a "normal couple".

Several factors affect sexual desire, including physical and emotional well-being, personal experiences, upbringing, convictions, lifestyle and even the current emotional status of the relationship. Certain common causes for low sex drive in women are – impact of some prescription drugs, especially anti-depressants, being chronically sleep-deprived, changes in hormonal levels, postpartum depression, etc.

Learnings:

1. Under the Indian Penal Code, a wife is presumed to consent to perpetual sex with her husband after getting married.

2. On one hand, the law protects all women from sexual violence; on the other hand it shields marital rape, although classified under domestic violence.

3. While marital rape has been recognised as a criminal offense in more than 100 countries, India, unfortunately falls among the 36 countries that have still not criminalised marital rape.

4. Section 375 of IPC (Indian Penal Code) defines rape as a criminal offence. By definition, rape is committed by a man if he has intercourse with a women without her consent or if she is below 18 years of age (a minor).

5. Exception 2 to Section 375 of the IPC exempts sexual intercourse with an unwilling wife, thus making it legal to have sex with his unwilling wife, which otherwise qualifies as rape.

A recent controversial judgement, passed by a single judge of Nagpur bench of the Bombay High Court on January 19, 2021, acquitted a man accused of groping a 12-year-old girl under the Protection of Children from Sexual Offences (POCSO) Act, 2012 which entails a minimum punishment of three years.

The 'disturbing' decision held that "there must be skin to skin contact with sexual intent" for an act to be considered sexual assault. Since the accused had groped the minor without removing her clothes, the offence could not be termed as sexual assault but instead constituted the offence of outraging a woman's modesty, under IPC, Section 354, which entails a minimum sentence of up to one year.

The order could lead a dangerous trend.

CHILDHOOD TRAUMAS

GENDER JUMBLE

"Nature made a mistake, which I have corrected."
- Christine Jorgensen (An American transgender woman who was the first person to become widely known in the United States for having sex reassignment surgery way back in 1952)

Today's youth crave independence. Many households understand this and provide kids the privacy and freedom they so obsessively demand. Often there are fights and emotional outbursts before parents finally give in. It is a tough call. If they don't, the child may rebel or even run away. If they do, the child could get into serious trouble and, what's worse, this time around with the sanction of the family.

A number of factors are at play here: the size of the house, the socio-economic background, the neighbourhood and the number of children in the household. If there are two or more kids, the rope is loosened depending on the age, emotional maturity and sense of responsibility of each child.

A rebellious teen is often uncontrollable and unwilling to listen to caution or reason. Peer pressure, a sense of coming-into-one's-own and raging hormones can drive them to great lengths to get what they want. The consequences can be disastrous. By the time they realise their mistake, it is often too late. A promising life can be scarred forever. The elders can see the future, having been through it all. But try explaining it to a rebellious teen!

Tina was a young, boisterous girl of 18. Smart, good-looking, fashionable and well-groomed, she came from a well-off family. A good student and gregarious, she was popular both with her classmates and the college faculty. Bina, her younger sister, who studied in the same college, was equally studious but not as popular. Taller, also attractive in her own way, she was shy and introverted. She loved being by herself and was reserved with strangers. The two sisters were often referred to as the 'two poles' in their social circle.

But Bina was very protective of her elder sister and chaperoned her wherever she went.

Tina found Bina's over-protective nature suffocating and inhibiting. She advised her to create her own circle of friends, and get a life of her own. But Bina would just wander away for a while and return to hover around Tina. The only time Tina could escape her sister's cloying attention, was in the gym. She was into physical fitness and never missed a session. With time, she developed a chiselled, muscular physique adding to her allure and popularity.

As the years passed, Tina's ambition was to get away from home and study in some college abroad. "I used to feel claustrophobic," she confessed. "But I couldn't disclose this to anyone in my family. I just wanted to get away and create a new life for myself."

Both the sisters shared a room. They even shared their podcasts, music and bed, to "snuggle in" at times. As kids, they shared a lot of bonhomie and even showered together. But as they grew up and matured, things changed. Bina started distancing herself from her sister. Tina found it strange at first, but then accepted it. Bina was younger, still growing up, but suddenly seemed to be physically awkward. This seemed unusual.

By now, Tina had firmly decided to seek admission to a foreign university. She often wondered about Bina. Her behaviour was definitely offbeat and she seemed so different from the other girls. She was definitely hiding something. But since she didn't talk about it, Tina couldn't lay a finger on what was wrong.

Although curious, Tina resisted confronting her sister. She had some suspicions, but she let them be as they were unfounded. She tried to talk to her parents about this but they didn't see anything strange in Bina's behaviour. With time, Bina became totally introverted and a recluse. She did well in her studies, which overshadowed everything else. Her parents were overjoyed with her academic progress and even rebuked Tina for misunderstanding her sister.

Meanwhile, Tina consulted a career counsellor and opted to go to the UK for further studies. Managing to get admission to a college in the UK was not difficult as she had good grades in college and had scored well in her SAT and GRE examinations.

She did face some resistance from her parents when she broke the news to them. Bina was also very hurt. But Tina knew in her heart that she was making the right move. Bina's strange behaviour was getting worse. She seemed uncomfortable with her changing body and was averse to confiding in Tina. Some distance between them was absolutely essential now.

Going abroad on her own had its risks. New friends, a new place, unfamiliar surroundings and a whole new world called out. It was both exciting and frightening.

Finally, she secured admission in a college in the UK, around August 2019. The first few months were devoted to settling down and understanding a new culture. She had a pretty Irish girl as her roommate who had a boyfriend, and spent more time outside with him than in the room.

Tina was used to the Indian hustle and bustle. Suddenly, life was completely different. She started taking long walks after classes and moved around the city to understand it better and get acclimatised. London was dark, cold and lonely. Tina started missing her family, especially Bina, who had been her constant companion for many years.

By December, London had become terribly cold and gloomy. Tina's loneliness and alienation grew worse as her roommate decided to take a drop from college and go back home to Ireland. Through Christmas and New Year, Tina was all by herself. She felt desolate. The college had also shut down for the holidays and she was left to her own devices.

But, thankfully, when college reopened in January, she had a new roommate and was delighted to have some company. But there was a surprise in store. Her roommate, a tall well-built girl from Germany, didn't know much English. In one of her conversations, she confessed that she was attracted to girls and that she found Tina very beautiful. All this was shocking for Tina as she had never been exposed to any form of alternate sexuality. She was still trying to find her feet in a new country and now was being propositioned by a stranger of the same gender! She didn't know how to react. She was scared and wanted to run back to home and family.

Then COVID-19 and the lockdown happened...

Tina first approached *HalloHappiness* in early March as she was unsure of her feelings towards Martina, her German roommate, named after the famous tennis player Martina Navratilova. She was in a quandary. She wanted to talk.

Martina was a simple, honest and hardworking girl who was struggling with her gender confusion. She wanted to be in the UK because the LGBTQ laws had been in force since July 2013, while in Germany they came into force only in October 2017. "This makes a difference in people's mindset, as there is much less acceptance back home in Germany for Martina," Tina explained.

Tina admitted to us that she had decided to quit studies and return home as she was lonely and missing her family. After a few conversations we convinced her not to do that. She had gone there after a lot of preparation and struggle. There would be difficulties in the initial stages but once she adjusted, life would be beautiful. She had to hang on. Tina listened to us and stayed back to complete her studies.

We also told her that Martina's situation was beyond her control and not to agonise about it. All she needed to do was extend her emotional support. Later, she also made Martina talk to us. Martina opened up and discussed her situation candidly. This also helped Tina understand Martina better. They became the best of friends. Tina also took the initiative to get Martina to speak to Bina, and it was confirmed that Bina too had a gender identity crisis. They shared notes and Tina promised to help her out once she returned.

Tina called us again after the lockdown was announced. She was stuck in the UK as flights were suspended due to the pandemic. She laughed at the irony. "It is as though God is teaching me a prolonged lesson. I was desperate to get out of home and came to the UK, pondered going back, then decided not to, and now I am stuck here." She had also begun to spend more time with Martina and understood her well. "I have grown very fond of her. I can fully understand her apprehensions and trauma. She is now keen on a surgery and wants to live as a normal man. She laughingly says that she will change her name to Martin after surgery, which will be easy on the passport as only one letter has to be deleted. How cool is that?"

Having been exposed to alternate sexuality, Tina was now fully prepared to help Bina. She understood Bina's strange behaviour as it was tough to 'come out' in a conservative Indian milieu; one could be misunderstood and ridiculed. "I am ready to support Bina, as I understand her struggles much better now. Maybe I needed to understand life and that's the reason I had to travel all the way to the UK. My bond with my family, especially Bina, has become very strong now. I miss all of them."

Tina's need for independence and the move away from her family worked out well for her. The exposure broadened her outlook and contributed to her growth. She was keen to talk to her sister openly once she got back, and help find a solution. She knew it would be tough, given the social conditions, as well as her parents' mind-set. But she was determined to find a way out. "I want to see Bina happy after all her struggles. That is all."

A lot has changed in recent times for the LGBTQ community. Friendly laws have been passed and the lay public sensitised to their needs. It is a long road ahead but a start has been made.

Learnings:

1. Sexual preferences are personal issues and often hidden. To accept a perceived deviation without judgement or ridicule, people's mindsets need to change. It will take time.

2. Having said that, many favourable changes have taken place. Laws have been enacted and the lay public sensitised. Acceptance for the LGBTQ community has increased worldwide after several landmark judgements in favour of same-sex marriages and relationships. More laws need to be enacted, especially in the workplace, to make the path easier for them.

3. Social acceptance of different sexual orientations and gender identities should be complete and non-discriminatory.

4. Anti-bullying policies, at each age group, can serve as a deterrent. Schools, colleges and workspaces need to be insulated from gender animosity and sensitised to new gender equations.

5. A new class of psychiatrists and counsellors, trained specifically in alternate sexuality issues, will be in great demand. Doctors too, for sex reassignment surgeries.

6. Gender and sexuality issues have now come to stay as an integral part of Indian society. The sooner we accept it, the better for all of us.

THE UNENDING TRAUMA OF CHILD SEX ABUSE

> "Anything that's human is mentionable, and anything that is mentionable can be more manageable. When we can talk about our feelings, they become less overwhelming, less upsetting and less scary. The people we trust with that important talk can help us know that we are not alone."
> *- Fred Rogers*

Life sometimes subjects us to trauma which we are unable to control, express or forget. As children, our impressionable and innocent minds are assailed by all sorts of images and incidents that can harm us and create emotional trauma, which remains and ferments in our subconscious well into adulthood.

Vibhuti contacted us sometime in January 2020. I could only hear her sobs and not her words. I tried to strain my ears to comprehend what she was trying to tell me but after a while realised that she was expressing her anguish through tears; no words were spoken.

She calmed down later but still couldn't speak. I allowed her to sit back, contemplate for a while whatever she wanted to share, and persuaded her to speak without inhibition. I convinced her that everything she said would be confidential. It was obvious that she was deeply stressed by some very personal experience, and the trauma was too great to share easily. I knew that she wanted to talk. So I just gave her time.

Vibhuti's story unfolded over a number of sessions as it was difficult for her to articulate her feelings.

Daughter of an officer in the Central services of Union Government, she and Vaibhav, her elder brother, spent their childhood in different parts of Uttar Pradesh and Delhi. Most of her early childhood was spent in palatial houses provided by the government. They lived well, with a retinue of domestic help allocated to senior officers. She later attended college in Delhi and lived in a well-appointed apartment, in a posh locality. It was a middle-class upbringing.

"I have always been a quiet girl," she opened up. "As a child I did not have any company. My brother, Vaibhav, is ten years older than me. He had his own group of friends and never encouraged me to hang around with them. He was already a teenager when I started going to school. Maybe, I was an afterthought, or an accident," she said with a half-smile in her voice.

"My mother was a school teacher and would be out of the house most of the day, busy with work and her social life. As my school was close by, a rickshawwwala would pick me up and drop me back. I would go to my room after lunch, finish my homework and rest a bit. I was 5-years-old and all alone at home." Her school timings were from 9.30 am to 1.30 pm. Vaibhav and her mother would be back home by 4 pm and her father, much later, at around 8 pm. So, for a little over two hours, Vibhuti was alone at home everyday.

At this point, Vibhuti's voice started getting fainter. I could sense her anguish. She tried to talk but choked on her tears and started sobbing bitterly. Slowly, it all unfolded; the trauma that she had undergone as a child. It took a lot of courage for her to reveal that she had been sexually abused by the domestic help.

The younger help noticed that she was home alone every day for about two hours and seized the opportunity. Vibhuti was too young to understand what was happening. All she knew was that she hated what was being done to her. This assault on her continued. When the older help realised what was happening, instead of complaining and exposing the goings-on, he too joined in.

"It was a torture, but being a quiet and shy girl, I couldn't muster enough courage to talk about this to anyone. This lasted for about three months until my father got transferred." Vibhuti kept her secret. No one knew of this shameful act. She suffered in silence. She believed that she was the one responsible for what she had gone through, and that added to her torment.

"As I grew older, I started feeling very guilty for having been subjected to such humiliation and not having the courage to tell anyone," continued Vibhuti. "I became quieter and would spend hours alone in my room. As I was a quiet child by nature, nobody noticed the difference. Also, my grades kept improving as books were my only companion. So no one suspected that anything was amiss. All they saw were my excellent grades."

Meanwhile, Vibhuti got close to a girl named Bela, her new friend in class. She was free-spirited and like all girls her age, would incessantly talk about boys. She found it unusual that Vibhuti showed no interest in the opposite gender but left it at that. "With time, I grew comfortable in this friendship and finally, after years of living in a hell of my own making, I narrated the incident to her," confessed Vibhuti. "Bela was shocked and couldn't believe that I had kept this a secret for so many years and lived with the guilt. She encouraged me to confide in my mother, as my parents had a right to know the truth. She insisted that action had to be taken against the two domestic help.

"I finally mustered the courage to narrate the incident to my mother but was taken aback by her reaction. She told me never to open my mouth again to anyone, and to keep this a secret. She also did not think it necessary to counsel me or show any sympathy for the trauma I had gone through. I was shocked. She wanted me to behave as though nothing had happened."

Her mother thought that it was no use digging up the past. She also didn't want to make an official complaint, or even tell Vibhuti's father about what had happened. "It will only give you a bad name if we make an official complaint," was her reaction. "Since I was expecting sympathy and some action and got nothing, I withdrew further into my shell. Bela tried her best to uplift my sagging spirits but she also gave up after a while. I was left to indulge in self-pity. I had to push back those memories and books became my salvation. As a result, I excelled in studies, and earned kudos for my high marks. That helped me regain some self-confidence."

After she graduated, Vibhuti's parents started to hunt for a suitable groom for her. She had never had a boyfriend or shown any interest in boys till then. Finally, a suitable boy was found, and Vibhuti was married off as soon as she completed her postgraduate studies.

"My husband, Saurabh, runs a family business of three generations and being the only child and heir to the business, our marriage was a grand affair," Vibhuti recounted. "Everybody was elated and the celebrations lasted a week. I tried to be involved and feel happy as I was starting a new chapter of my life. But I just couldn't think of the future as harmonious, considering what I had gone through. I had several doubts in my mind about being able to conduct the physical part of my marriage, but didn't have anyone to talk to, or share my apprehensions with. My mother pretended as though nothing untoward had ever happened to me and that put me in a further dilemma. When I tried to broach the subject, she shut me down with a 'You haven't forgotten about it?' I was helpless."

Vibhuti got married in December 2019 and shifted to her husband's home. It was a joint family and the celebrations continued. There were a lot of people around, so no time or space for marital intimacy. Vibhuti was busy looking after the household and catering to the guests as her mother-in-law wanted to showcase her as the new acquisition in the family. Saurabh was also busy with the family celebrations and the business.

But the day finally arrived. "I froze at his intimate touch," admitted Vibhuti. Saurabh did not take it amiss the first time, thinking that she may need some time to open up. "Things started to get worse when the situation repeated a few times. However, Saurabh remained patient and understanding. He noticed that I was shy and would cry. So, he didn't push me."

After marriage Saurabh took some time off from work and started working from home and had plenty of time. "But whenever he came close, or tried to speak about my attitude towards intimacy, I would start crying," continued Vibhuti. "He had been patient and understanding till now but since my only response to his overtures was crying, he felt helpless. This was a great opportunity for us to get to know each other better but instead, we were growing apart."

That's when Vibhuti got in touch with us. I could sense that unloading the trauma she had been nursing for years, was a great relief to her. Bottling up her anguish and sense of violation had led to feelings of guilt and negativity. Whenever she had spoken about her situation to her mother, she had been told to keep quiet. So she was petrified of sharing the unsavoury details of her life with anyone, more so with a complete stranger.

But for the first time, she got a non-judgemental response to her story and that encouraged her to spill it all out.

We counselled her. We told her not to feel guilty or wronged as she had done nothing wrong and it wasn't her fault at all. In fact it was a deeper trauma for her as she was a child when it happened. We told her that life is an offering and that she should leave her past behind and move ahead.

We also counselled her husband. He was an understanding and kind man and was shocked when he heard her story for the first time and he extended his complete support. Saurabh's reaction was a great relief for Vibhuti. They resolved the issue together and forged a greater bond. The marriage started working out.

She called us later, just to tell us how she had finally been able to bury her demons and was now looking forward to a long and happy married life with a very understanding partner.

The World Health Organisation (WHO) defines child sexual abuse (CSA) as: "The involvement of a child in sexual activity that he or she does not fully comprehend, is unable to give informed consent to, or for which the child is not developmentally prepared and cannot give consent, or that violates the laws or social taboos of society." CSA includes an array of sexual activities like fondling, inviting a child to touch or be touched sexually, intercourse, exhibitionism, involving a child in prostitution or pornography, or online child luring by cyber-predators.

CSA is a serious problem, of considerable magnitude throughout the world.

Incest, another form of physical abuse where the perpetrator is a close family member, is highly underreported in patriarchal societies.

CSA has profound consequences for the child. It is known to interfere with the growth and development of the child and is linked to numerous maladaptive health behaviours and poor social, mental and physical outcomes throughout life.

Large-scale studies conducted in India have uncovered alarming numbers of child sex abuse. It is a situation that has to be snuffed out as soon as possible. Many laws have been enacted with that end in mind.

Learnings:

1. Most child sexual abuse goes unreported. So all figures are only the tip of the iceberg.

2. It is extremely important to be empathetic to the child as this is a situation of deep trauma.

3. Parents, caught up in their busy lives these days, tend to neglect such issues.

4. It is the primary responsibility of parents to keep close bonds with their pre-adolescent children and practice necessary safeguards for their well-being. They should be able to sensitise children about 'bad touch' and encourage them to bring it to their notice immediately, be it from a family member, family friend, household help, school bus conductor or even a stranger.

5. All such incidents should be reported to the authorities and perpetrators must be punished severely.

6. The affected child must receive proper counselling immediately so that the trauma doesn't distort his/her adult life.

7. POCSO (Protection of Children from Sexual Offences) Act 2012, is a comprehensive law for the protection of children from offences of sexual assault, sexual harassment and pornography. It requires special treatment of cases relating to child sexual abuse such as setting-up of special courts, special prosecutors and support persons for child victims.

8. Treatment of a child who is a victim of incest, requires a biopsychosocial approach as the trauma can be very deep.

It's advisable to involve medical professionals in case of deep physical injury.

THE ABANDONED CHILD

"Early relational trauma results from the fact that we are often given more to experience in this life than we can bear to experience consciously. This problem has been around since the beginning of time, but it is especially acute in early childhood where, because of the immaturity of the psyche and/or brain, we are ill-equipped to metabolize our experience. An infant or young child who is abused, violated or seriously neglected by a caretaking adult, is overwhelmed by intolerable affects that are impossible for it to metabolize, much less understand or even think about."
- Donald Kalsched (Trauma and the Soul: A Psycho-spiritual Approach to Human Development and its Interruption)

What do you say to a 16-year-old who feels that he has never been loved? It's tough to respond to such an emotional void since almost everyone is loved by their parents. At least, that is the universal perception and accepted truth. Rarely, if at all, is a child emotionally abandoned.

In our experience as counsellors, we come across a number of relationship issues which primarily stem from misunderstanding or poor communication. More often than not, it is the sensitive ones who fall into this trap as they are unable to negotiate perceived pain or hurt. They are also poor communicators and tighten the lid on their emotions, fearing further hurt. They are the biggest sufferers, as others, emotionally stronger, move on quickly, dusting aside their many failures. Unfortunately, the world can be particularly unkind to the meek, who are also genuine givers. But then, life is a battle for survival. When the going gets tough, the tough have to get going!

Sid's great sorrow was the belief that he had never been loved in his life. His story unfolded over a number of conversations. Although in a hurry to offload his trauma, he was unable to articulate his thoughts in a coherent manner. Slowly, our soft nudges of approval and encouragement helped him open up. From his early childhood memories and the first incident that torched his soul, to the impressions that led to his present dilemma.

Sid recalled his fifth birthday. Being the first male child in a large family that included all his cousins, his birthday was celebrated on a grand scale. In between the festivities, he overheard a conversation between his parents. They were having a showdown behind closed doors.

His mother was yelling at his father, "I never wanted a child so soon because I was keen to devote a few more years to my career. But your obsession with your family, and one mistake from me, and here he is." She walked out slamming the door. Her parting shot hit

Sid in the gut, "Why don't you look after him instead of jet-setting for your business? What does it leave me with?" His father, equally angry, yelled back, "Why have a child at all if you are so conscious of your figure and career?"

Sid has never forgotten those hurtful words ever since.

He recounted the story of his parents' courtship. His father met his mother on a flight. She was a beauty and he fell for her physical attributes. He had tasted early material success and, goaded by his mother, was in a hurry to settle down. He came from a large family and all the other siblings were married and had kids. So there seemed little reason for him to continue being single. Although not classically handsome, he carried himself with confidence. She was keen on a career in films or the fashion industry. Marriage was an option. They met frequently, one thing led to another and they tied the knot within three months. Not much later, Sid was born.

Feeling neglected at home, Sid recalled all his attention-drawing techniques. He went from being naughty to impertinent, and finally, unmanageable. While his father was often away travelling for work, his mother indulged all the fancy demands he made. The focus was never on studies as he believed that showing no interest in books was the best form of defiance.

His grades kept falling. There were constant arguments between his parents on how badly he was being raised. His mother seemed constantly on her guard as she was blamed by his father for his every single failing, and Sid was always at the receiving end. The final straw was when they decided to send him to a boarding school. That seemed to be the solution to all the problems at home.

Sid was not even ten!

"I was a popular and perfectly charming boy outside my home as I did not feel the need to catch anyone's attention," explained Sid. "People loved me for who I was. I was a bright and well-behaved child for everyone else. Home and school were the only places where I was looking for approval, as the atmosphere was becoming increasingly disapproving and claustrophobic. I was only looking for some emotional support from my family, so being sent to a boarding school came as a jolt. I lost all confidence. I felt abandoned. But I had to act brave since I did not have any other place to go back to. At that age, your parents and home are all you have."

Life was a roller-coaster for Sid thereafter. "I would come back sometimes to the place called 'home' during the holidays," he continued. "My parents tried to show me their love and affection since I was a visitor now, but I had no love for them. I felt emotionally cheated as a child. I have gone through one relationship, which did not last because I feared rejection and couldn't open up. It is possibly because I overheard my mother saying that she didn't want me. I am lonely in my core and wish I wasn't born. I want a close relationship, but am unable to have one, as I fear rejection and abandonment.

"Currently, I am spending a few months at home. But I am unhappy within and want to run away. I am applying to universities outside India. I would be happy to be away from home, with friends. Sid added a parting shot, "I will never send my children to a boarding school."

Primarily, not just children, but even adults, are looking for unconditional love and acceptance, a validation for who they are. It is often overlooked and leads to complicated, misunderstood relationships.

At *HalloHappiness* we explained to Sid the necessity to bridge his relationship with his parents, as nothing in life is permanent and situations change all the time. What he overheard as a child should not be misread as an absolute statement of rejection. Given a chance, they may have a perfect explanation for their exchanges on that fateful day. Couples fight and say nasty things to each other. This may have been just a one-off angry exchange.

Our counselling helped him understand the situation but the real healing will come once he has an open dialogue with his parents. He was encouraged by our explanations, but Sid had yet to start that dialogue as his parents probably didn't even know the trauma that was crusting his soul all these years.

Unfortunately, his parents were not our clients. It was also not in our purview to approach them. So, unless he initiated a sharing of thoughts and emotions, the stalemate would continue, and Sid would continue to suffer the disturbing onslaught of a childhood memory.

Learnings:

1. In bigger cities, the lack of space at home needs to be considered while dealing with emotional issues between husband and wife. Often, the problem is nothing more serious than intense and prolonged proximity, or lack of communication and boredom for one partner.

2. Parents need to encourage their children to be free and openly discuss issues. It is also advisable to be extra observant to understand their child's psyche as they are exposed to an overload of information via social media. This could have an adverse impact.

3. Conflicts are an integral part of adult life. But they need to be addressed with civility, especially if there is a child at home. Parents and elders leave lasting impressions on children.

4. When parents notice a distinct rebellion in a child, leading to prolonged discord in the family, it is advisable to enlist outside help of counsellors. Early intervention is the key to success, as any thought harboured for long, gets embedded in the psyche.

HEALING PARENT-CHILD DISCORD

"All parents damage their children. It cannot be helped. Youth, like pristine glass, absorbs the prints of its handlers. Some parents smudge, others crack, a few shatter childhoods completely into jagged little pieces, beyond repair."
- Mitch Albom (The Five People You Meet in Heaven)

The fine notion of instilling discipline in children can be a nightmare for both parents and children. Kids are different, situations are different and the same punitive disciplinary tactics do not necessarily work across the board.

Minal, in her first session with *HalloHappiness*, was quite outspoken about her emotions towards her family, especially her parents. She was convinced that they had been particularly favourable to Dinesh, her younger brother. She disliked them for their preferential treatment, which had also created a wedge between the siblings. She approached us to get an objective view of her circumstances since she was visiting her family after a break of six years, during which there had been no communication between them.

It all began many years ago. The daily arguments with her parents, restrictions imposed and several other unsavoury incidents, pushed her to desperately want to leave home. While she blamed her parents, Minal admitted sheepishly that she had also been rude and irresponsible. It was not that she was entirely innocent and at the receiving end all the time.

After finishing her postgraduate studies in Microbiology, Minal was able to procure a job in a pharmaceutical company in Singapore, in a junior research team. Her ticket to freedom came sooner than she had expected, and she grabbed it. Her friend, Renu, was working for the same company and helped her out with boarding and lodging. Both were single and enjoyed each other's company. So, the arrangement worked well. Renu was two years older and quite protective of Minal. She in turn, was grateful to Minal for the emotional support. It was a perfect arrangement for two young girls, away from home, working in a foreign country.

Minal had arrived home for her parents' 50th wedding anniversary, which was being celebrated on a grand scale. She had, over the years, reconciled to some of the seemingly unfair domestic incidents imprinted in her psyche. But what still festered was her own sense of inadequacy and self-worth.

Minal was also facing issues in her personal relationships. At 30, she was finding it difficult to be intimate with any boy as her parents' volatile marriage had scarred her; the images of marriage were always unpleasant. She was apprehensive about her ability to handle a close relationship. "I have a fierce temper," she admitted. "It is difficult to keep calm when I don't have it my way, and relationships are all about compromises."

She wanted us to validate her decision to visit the family as she did not want to reopen the wounds she had so meticulously worked at closing. It is difficult to affirm or decry a human action, especially if it has a long, unaddressed history. Time does heal wounds. In most cases, both sides are to blame. We tried our best to help her sort out the situation.

Parents also go through their own dilemma; the more docile and agreeable child is always bestowed extra benefits, liberties and cuddles. Minal admitted that she was the more difficult child, being aggressive, short-tempered and demanding. Her brother Dinesh, was the saner, sober child in the family and everyone's darling. He was the model child. Undemanding, scoring good grades, fairly good in sports and the favourite of his school teachers, Dinesh received all the applause. But Minal's point was that parents, as elders, should be able to understand the needs of children and deal with them at separate levels.

In counselling, we have seen irrevocable differences between parents and children. Sometimes, the differences are never addressed. Buckling under the pressures of handling kids, parents are drained of their energies and often lose objectivity. Lapses in communication do happen.

Minal revealed that her parents had been approaching her to reconnect. They wanted to be forgiven if they had inadvertently hurt her. But Minal was unable to take the first step towards reconciliation.

Depending on the sensitivity of the child, and sometimes the parents, it can take months or sometimes years to see eye-to-eye, or it may never even happen at all. In some cases, the parents even pass on, taking unresolved issues to the grave.

In such cases, it is best to speak to a professional counsellor and get an objective view. Minal took our advice and decided to revisit the past to exorcise the demons lurking in her psyche. We encouraged her to take the first step.

It was most rewarding to hear her cheerful voice when she returned to Singapore. She had been able to bury her bitter past, and make peace all around. She had also become friends with her younger brother. In fact, over a period of time, she became a loving daughter and sister once again.

In close relationships, objectivity is often the first casualty, as emotions run high. Seeking counselling is the easiest solution because sometimes, neutral, outside eyes, are necessary to repair a broken family.

Learnings:

1. Children need careful nurturing, at least till the impressionable age of ten.

2. Parent-child discord is the most unsettling emotion in families, and quite common. There is no simple solution other than to be understanding of a child's anxieties and putting them to rest. Enlisting help from outside counsellors is productive, as it provides an emotional outlet for both, instead of direct confrontation.

3. The emotional buffer provided by joint families is often lacking in nuclear families, so some amount of friction is a given. It is important to protect children from any apparent discord between parents.

4. It is advisable not to nurture grief for too long as it can fester and damage the physical, emotional and spiritual body. It is important to release that grief by speaking to someone trustworthy. Or to address the root cause and get closure. Sometimes, there is no solution. Then, one just has to move on without looking back.

YOUTH ADDICTIONS

YOUTH, DRUGS AND DECADENCE

"Youth is a dream, a form of chemical madness."
- F. Scott Fitzgerald (Tales of the Jazz Age)

Ruchika arrived in Mumbai as a student. To be 16, full of life and in the most happening city of India is a dream come true for any youngster. Mumbai boasts a freedom for its citizens, unrivalled by any other part of the country. For women, it is the one of the safest cities, day or night.

Like her peers, Ruchika rented a tiny apartment with two other girls. Since she was new to the city and didn't know anyone, most of her free time was spent with her apartment mates. They would hang out together, go for movies and late night ice-creams and throng the usual places teenagers frequent. They were all from financially comfortable backgrounds and so there was enough money to splurge.

With time, they befriended some boys to hang out with. One late evening, one of the boys challenged them to consume something stronger than their regular intoxicants. They accepted the challenge, and their world changed after that. It literally went up in smoke. A major drug addiction study suggests that majority of addicts are introduced to drugs by friends and 35 percent continue the practice after trying out drugs out of curiosity, daring and fun.

Soon, the boys started visiting their pad often. They brought along their friends too, one thing led to another, and their apartment became a weekend party joint. Youth, hormones, intoxicants and enough money to fuel every fantasy in smoke rings, took over their young lives.

As the months passed, college attendance fell, grades plummeted and life turned directionless. One day, out of sheer curiosity, one of the parents visited unannounced. He was shocked by what he saw. He rebuked his daughter and whisked her away. But, for some strange reason, he didn't think it was appropriate to alert the other parents about the situation.

Ruchika and Aabha, her other flatmate, got further sucked into this life of drugs and dissipation. They fell headlong into a web of lies, cunning and deceit. Their needs increased, their plunge into decadence was on overdrive and with rising expenses, they had to find other methods to support their lifestyle.

Life also threw up new potholes. They were in for a rude shock when they realised that the boys, who had become their best friends, had duped them. They had amassed huge debts and hurriedly left the scene, leaving the girls to pay off their creditors. The girls were in a fix. There seemed no escape and no going back. Over time, they managed to accrue the money and pay off the guys who came threatening to their doorstep. It was a terrible situation, and Ruchika and Aabha had learnt the lesson of their lives.

Ruchika's first call to us was a 'no call', in the sense that she didn't utter a single word. All we heard was sobbing at the other end. And after crying for a while there was nothingness, just bleak, eerie silence. She called again a few days later and mustered the courage to talk. She told us about her irresponsible behaviour and the guilt she bore from years of taking for granted the trust of her family, her life and her body.

She was only 19. She had come to Mumbai three years earlier with stars in her eyes and the promise of a wonderful future. She wanted to pursue her ambitions and dreams, and not end up a doped wreck. Aabha too was in introspection mode. They both knew that they had thrown the opportunity of a great life into the gutter. They had youth, looks, intelligence, money and family backup and yet they had foolishly blown it all away. They didn't know what to do, how to survive, how to face society, how to retrieve lost time and even contemplated suicide. The only thing that held them back was the family's reputation, which would have been further ruined if they did something so drastic.

Their main concern now was how to face their families. They had failed their love and trust. They kept repeating, "Our parents gave us everything we asked for. They trusted us completely, loved us unconditionally, sent us money whenever we wanted it, unquestioningly. We lacked nothing. So what made us do all this, ruin our careers and life?" There were no answers. These are individual choices and every single human being bears the burden of choice.

Fortunately, in this case, their introspection and the forced self-imposed isolation due to their own guilt and fear helped. They couldn't meet anyone and used the time to seek solutions. They were at a crossroad and had to make the right decisions now. Another mistake and it would be a complete disaster.

They called us regularly and our assurances and non-judgemental attitude helped them, not only to come to terms with their situation, but also to regain some of their lost confidence. "I was the shy, quiet kid in the house, and never had to deal with the outside world," confessed Ruchika. "Everything I needed was provided for, and my brothers and father were extremely protective of me. I simply cannot understand how I could have been so foolish and got into drugs and do all that I did?"

Aabha had her own explanation. "I was the tomboy and outgoing kid in the family, and everyone, including me, thought I could handle any situation. So, when these boys approached us, I was confident of managing the outcome. I was obviously overconfident, which I realised later, much to my peril." Both Ruchika and Aabha were torn by guilt. They were filled with remorse, came down heavily on themselves and desperately wanted to change the track of their lives. That realisation was a vital starting point for recovery.

We listened to them quietly and allowed them to vent, to go through the myriad emotions they were feeling. All we did was to offer a kind ear, without judgement. They had realised their mistake and didn't need any further shaming.

Despite, or probably because of, all their exposure to social media and the overload of information floating around, today's youth are caught up in conflicting directions. The material world is filled with goodies and distractions, and life is too short and fast to taste it all. Youth is also fleeting. As the Yanks once said in the glory days of free sex and rock and roll, "Live fast, die young."

When one is young, it is easy to make mistakes in a hurry and repent at leisure. This is where parents need to step in. Unconditional love, without proper parental guidance and controls, is detrimental to the child. Parents need to set examples and maybe draw the line with some clarity and force.

Communication and open dialogue between generations is necessary. Children, parents and grandparents have to bond. There is wisdom in years and it has to be passed down gently and diplomatically. Your child should be able to come back to you and say, "Hey dad/mom, I messed up. Will life give me another chance? Will you?" And the parent should be able to hug the child and say firmly, "YES, of course." Today's generation is extremely bright. A little guidance will set them off in the right direction.

Learnings:

1. Communication is the greatest bridge in any relationship. Between parent and child, it is paramount. Open dialogue should be the key to demolish any misunderstanding.

2. Building trust all over again and not shaming the child is necessary. The scars of teenage years shouldn't cast a shadow on one's entire life. These are passing phases and should be left behind. Spilt milk can never be recovered. Let it be.

3. Parents are also conditioned by the pressures of society and often unnecessarily admonish the child. While peer and societal pressures have their role to play, parents have to bend a bit and accommodate their offspring with complete trust. They have gone through the same period in their lives and know the pitfalls. Times have changed but the basic and core instincts remain the same. Forgiveness without judgement, and a new positive path, should be charted out.

4. Joint families are breaking up and children leave home early, either for education or for a livelihood. They will face all sorts of challenges. The family should be the bedrock of values. A child should be rooted in its indigenous culture and not succumb to imported value systems. This is the responsibility of the parents.

5. Drugs, sex and a whole lot of psychedelic escape routes are common. There is a globalisation of 'sin'. The descent is very easy. Parents, friends and extended family have an important role to play. Healthy habits like sports, yoga, the right books and hobbies and proper nutrition should be inculcated early.

6. Counsellors have a critical role to play in shaping tomorrow.

THE ENSLAVING TENTACLES OF PORNOGRAPHY

"The porn that is being produced and sold to us is full of ideas and beliefs that are completely distorted, and that are in fact, opposite of what real sex, love, and relationships are like. Loving-healthy relationships are built on respect, equality, honesty. But in porn, this is quite the contrary. There, love and sex are based on domination, control, disrespect, and violence. Sweet, affectionate, caring interaction doesn't sell, but degradation and abuse do. And there's something deeply disturbing and concerning about an industry who profits from that."

- Orge Castellano

Sex, as we all know, is not a topic that is easily discussed. Talking about it openly is still taboo in many sections of society. Parents rarely talk about it to children and all the information that is gleaned on the topic today is from the worldwide web. Sex has also become commercial and more easily available now. Online dating is huge and with the sex industry too making its oomph felt on the net, there is actually a glut of opportunities, along with dangers for the casual seeker.

HalloHappiness has received innumerable calls concerning pornography. That made us realise how widespread the malaise is, and the enormity of the social distress it is causing across age groups.

24-year-old Sanju was an internet pornography addict. He confessed that he was addicted to porn for over a decade. Hailing from an affluent business family of Mumbai, he had a comfortable life. "I received a lot of attention from girls since my school days and I was also attracted to them," he confessed. He had his own room at home and this made it easy to access whatever material he wanted, whenever he wanted. "It was easy for me as compared to my classmates, who shared their room with a sibling or two. They had no privacy at all. Sometimes, they had no access to the internet at night, which is the ideal time for such activity. I had no such problems."

Sanju began watching pornography after being bullied at school. Pornography was the rage, so you had to watch porn, and revel in it, to be counted. "Once I started, I began to enjoy it," he opened up. "My watch time kept increasing. I got more and more curious and it took longer to get the rush. Sometimes I wonder if I would have embarked on the porn journey, if there wasn't peer approval. Maybe, I was weak-willed and suffered from a lack of self-esteem during my teenage years. But I desperately wanted to belong, and this was a good ticket."

But over the years, Sanju has been shackled by porn. "Much as I would like to give it up, I can't," he imploded. "It is impacting my relationship with my family and girlfriend. I am nervous, irritable and feel sapped of energy most of the time and even my girlfriend has noticed that I have no enthusiasm for most things in life. Sometimes, I do wish I hadn't started on this journey. Unfortunately, regret cannot undo the damage."

We thought that it may be a good idea to have an open discussion with his girlfriend on this subject. Sanju had become a porn addict and she suspected it, and so group counselling could help. But Sanju wasn't keen as he thought his girlfriend would reject him. We tried to convince him and told him not to be too harsh and judgemental on himself. Very often in life, we shut doors by being limited in our approach and thought processes. It is necessary to open doors and be vulnerable, especially in emotional situations. It may bring down the turbulence.

An All-Consuming Addiction

"Whether electing abstinence from sex or choosing to engage in sex with multiple lovers, sexual empowerment is about making decisions which are right and safe and true for you."
- Miya Yamanouchi

Siddhartha, 45-years-old, was married for 15 years, with two children. Living in a satellite city around New Delhi, he had easy access to internet porn. "I come from a middle-class, conservative family and things like this were a big dare for me," he explained. "I got into watching porn while I was in college and living in the hostel. I don't know if internet porn was available at that time, but a number of adult magazines were. School and college hostels are big markets for pornography and even one magazine dropped in the dorm gets wide circulation.

"As a normal progression, I graduated to internet porn," he continued. "I had the time and accessibility. But when you live in a small apartment, there is never enough privacy, and so I had to lie a lot. My wife was aware of my habit, I couldn't hide it from her. She watched a bit with me, but didn't enjoy it, so I started watching it by myself. Over a period of time, I started spending more time on this activity. The negative effect started to dawn on me after years of watching porn. By then, I was addicted."

Matters came to a head and Siddharth's need for pornography became desperate and more intense. He was hooked and needed more and more of it all the time. It was his go-to drug. "I was unable to get a high even after watching a lot of porn, and it took a toll on my married life. I am seriously making an attempt to give up this addiction but am finding it very difficult. Regrettably, my elder son is also into watching porn, and I am unable to stop him since I feel guilty, and also fearful of his response. What if he knows about my habit?"

Over many conversations, and after a lot of time, we were able to convince Siddhartha to partner with his wife in de-addicting his son. We encouraged them to have open conversations at home. Very often, we do not give enough credit to our children, as we tend to judge them in a protective format as parents with our own insecurities. Teenagers need to be given their space and we forget that they have questions which nobody is providing answers for. A sure-shot remedy for most such family issues is to make your children your friends, with boundaries of parenthood intact. This leads to healthier relationships.

Both Sanju and Siddhartha confessed to facing the most challenging time of their lives. For the first time there was a serious attempt to quit the habit. We encouraged them, provided them all the possible emotional and spiritual support required and hoped that with determined effort, they would engineer an escape from porn's clutching tentacles.

Porn today, is what tobacco was in the decades between 1960 and 1990 – a global addiction. Porn is almost the syllabus for teaching sex to our kids. Today's kids will be tomorrow's decision-makers, and their curriculum should necessarily impart values. The continued impressions of porn will only dwarf their emotional and spiritual growth and result in dysfunctional adults, contributing to a broken society. So, the sooner the widespread impact of porn is tethered, the better.

According to studies, one-third of all internet traffic is porn, and every third child is watching it.

It needs to be emphasised that the sex that is visible on screen is in a controlled environment, with a lot of fancy technical support. It sells a fantasy and is far removed from reality. It can send all the wrong messages, resulting in serious gender, social, medical and sexual issues.

Internet porn is a phenomenon explained as the 'Coolidge effect' in which a man's arousal is greater when he is with different women. Sex can remain a dirty word, but it will help if the values concerning the act are clean.

In a study, 100 out of 250 bestselling movies on porn were analysed. It was found that every single movie had aggression, cuss words and abuses hurled against women. Porn has, in recent times, become more aggressive and humiliating and women are shown solely as objects of male desire. Such a depiction promotes widespread abuse of women, commercial prostitution and human trafficking. Even if it doesn't give you a physical disease, it can hurt you psychologically.

The role of women is under debate in all walks of life, but not in porn. It has remained the same. In fact, it has got more humiliating as physical and verbal aggression has peaked. Brain scans have shown that compulsive porn users have the same frequencies as drug addicts. Other experiments have compared symptoms of sexual arousal with Attention Deficit Hyperactivity Disorder (ADHD), depression, concentration issues and a host of other psychological problems.

On Reddit, a network of communities with a common interest to kick the porn addiction habit, a panic button was put up by NoFap (an anti-masturbation movement). It was used by 3,000 people on day one! Now the panic button is used millions of times a year. This movement has touched a lot of lives and is playing an invaluable role in bringing back healthy relationships to society.

Learnings:

1. The majority of porn users are below the age of 25. Kicking the habit is an ongoing process and a long-term effort.

2. The data retrieved on pornography addiction has thrown a lot of light on the socio-psychological changes that happen in close relationships because of it.

3. It is imperative that we start talking about porn in critical discussions now, as it has started warping the minds of the current generation.

4. For far too long the health consequences of porn have been ignored. It is time to study it scientifically and arrive at remedial measures.

5. The traditional view of male-female porn has to be reviewed. All sorts of unimaginable permutations and combinations are at play now, causing irreparable harm to young minds. Cybercrime will have to tackle this issue with urgency.

6. The great danger is that the sex industry has also gone online. Sexual disease is now rampant. Sex is a core instinct and difficult to confine. With the easy accessibility of sex, both online and offline, the education of all stakeholders is the only way out. In situations like a pandemic and a lockdown, when meeting others is difficult, cybersex and online porn get a stimulus. Then it becomes an addiction. Before this destroys minds and homes, intervention is mandatory.

LOSS OF LOVED ONES, NO CLOSURE

TRAUMA OF THE FINAL GOODBYE

"Don't grieve. Anything you lose comes round in another form."
- Rumi

Losing a loved one is inevitable. We all know we are going to die. But when death calls out to someone we love, it can be an irrevocable jolt.

Ramona, the only child of her parents, described the grief that consumed her at the age of 42. In a series of conversations with us, she disclosed the events that led to the most impactful day of her life.

Ramona's mother passed away while giving birth to her. Her father took on the role of both parents. He was extremely indulgent with his only child. He didn't want Ramona to ever feel the lack of a mother and allowed her every liberty. Ramona could get away with the "wildest of acts." She grew up to be big-built, fair, tall, indulged, happy and wealthy. Nobody ever saw her in a dress as a kid; she was a 'trouser-top' girl, pampered, chilled out, the ultimate tomboy.

Her lavish 5,000-square-feet house in South Mumbai, was her den while growing up. Hailing from the upper crust of Mumbai society, she lacked nothing. And as the years passed, the father-daughter relationship grew into a strong bond of friendship. Nothing in the world could separate them.

After her early education, her father wanted her to study at a prestigious ivy league university overseas, but Ramona would have none of it. She refused to live away from him even for a day. "And for him nothing took precedence over me as I was the centre of his existence, his entire world. In a way, I think he was happy that I didn't leave," mused Ramona.

Her father, Jamshed, had a successful import/export business. He did very well for himself and both father and daughter travelled the globe for business meetings, as well as vacations. Never did Jamshed allow his daughter to feel the lack of a mother's love. He was her world.

"We often discussed my marriage but I was neither prepared for a *ghar jamai* (a popular term for a son-in-law who lives in the wife's house), nor prepared to leave my father," explained Ramona. "We argued about this for many years but I was unrelenting, and then, as was expected of me, I joined the family business."

Father and daughter, being buddies, would spend quiet evenings sipping beer and listening to soft music when not attending loud business bashes. "Every now and then he would chastise me. He wanted me to settle down before something happened to him. I would laugh it off saying he had strong genes and nobody who is 70 is old these days," recalled Ramona.

But life had other plans.

It was a jolt that shook her core. "Never did I imagine that he would pass on the way he did. Nobody was prepared for COVID-19!" Torn by grief, a tearful Ramona relived the quick turn of events, "That fateful day I took him to hospital, never to see him again. While I was trying to find a bed for him there was no time to address my emotions. We couldn't even say our good byes to each other, which we had practiced humorously so many times when he was alive. He used to joke about his departure. 'Rumi, just the two of us now. Don't forget to say a proper goodbye to me, unlike your mother who went into the delivery room and never came out. My only solace was the chubby pinkish toy in my arms, which was you.' And, after all this, I couldn't even say goodbye! How can God be so unfair!"

Although she spoke in a composed voice, it was evident that Ramona needed to acknowledge and address her grief to avoid a complete breakdown. "My mother died giving birth to me. Life came full circle when my father died without a warning. I haven't had a chance to come to terms with the loss, or the realisation that I will never see him again. I have lost all desire to live now. What do I have to live for?" She kept repeating a death wish.

We reasoned with her that death was an inescapable reality and the sooner she addressed her situation, the better for her. But it took a long time for her to accept the demise of her father. She was in anguish and denial for months.

To accept the loss of a loved one is undoubtedly emotionally challenging, and counselling cannot provide an instant remedy. To overcome the challenge, one has to make friends with one's emotions. Meanwhile, adopting a daily routine, self-motivation techniques, setting goals, physical exercise, a support system of friends and extended family, counselling, yoga and some medication, depending on the situation, might help.

Learnings:

1. Losing a loved one is a painful experience, more so in COVID-19 times, as people grieved in loneliness. The bodies were not handed over to the relatives, which did not allow any closure.

2. It is best to get back into a routine as quickly as possible – work, exercise, gardening or any mundane activity, all can be therapeutic.

3. If you are left alone and have no family, adopting a pet works wonders, as they provide unconditional love and emotional support.

GRIEF, GUILT AND REGRET

"He was both everything I could ever want...
And nothing I could ever have..."
- Ranata Suzuki

We couldn't understand her clearly when she first called. She had a soft, musical voice and spoke with an oriental accent, in between quiet sobs. It took us a while to decipher what she was saying.

Her name was Akiara. She was Japanese, and on a month-long trip to India "in search of peace". She planned to travel to various Buddhist pilgrim spots like Lumbini, Sarnath-Varanasi, Bodh Gaya and so on. She had just broken off from her long-term boyfriend and needed some 'me time' to reconstruct her life. Tall for a Japanese girl at 5'3", slim and fair, Akiara looked much younger than her 30 years.

She and her boyfriend had often contemplated visiting India, but never did. After the split, she decided to make the trip on her own to overcome the post-breakup blues. She visited a few pilgrim centres and the peace and tranquillity helped reduce the intensity of her grief. She felt better, was happier and was able to accept her situation. She was finally in a comfortable space.

But, once again, strange are the ways of destiny.

As Akiara was beginning to distance herself from the events of the past, she heard from her friends in Japan that her former boyfriend was seriously ill and hospitalised. The beautiful moments spent with him returned to haunt her. She lost her newly acquired tranquillity and slipped headlong into an emotional whirl. Consumed by guilt, she blamed herself, wanted to make amends for her imagined mistakes, and decided to fly back to Tokyo immediately.

Then COVID-19 and the subsequent lockdown imposing travel restrictions, added to her woes. Her frail emotional state, which was on the mend, was shattered again.

Akiara was torn between guilt and self-doubt. "I had actually prayed for peace in both our lives even though we had separated," she cried. "I was planning to see him on my return with a small gift from India, as he was so keen to come here. I have been so much at peace here, and have been able to arrive at some closure. But his sudden hospitalisation has opened a torrent of emotions in me, and I realise that I am still not over that chapter of my life. I am back to square one. Was it because of me that he fell sick?" Akiara was full of remorse.

Since air travel was not possible, she was dependent on her friends in Japan for updates. With no end to the lockdown in sight, Akiara grew more desperate.

On one of her calls to us she cried her heart out. "I feel that he is no more though my friends are saying that he is hospitalised. I am sure that he is no more." Her fears weren't unfounded. A few days later she got the confirmation of his death. She was inconsolable. When she called the next time, she just couldn't accept what had happened. She insisted that it was because of her that her former boyfriend had died.

We advised her to stay on in India. She was in no state to travel and anyway, there were no flights available. Finally, she returned to Japan when skeletal flights resumed, but kept calling us saying she would return to India in quest of the peace she had tasted.

Losing a loved one is an inevitability that we are rarely prepared for. The intensity of emotions leaves us powerless. Rituals help prepare the departed for the journey onward, and those left behind feel assuaged by the ceremonies. But, unfortunately, the COVID-19 restrictions did not leave room even for that. Not being able to perform last rites, or even see the bodies of their loved ones for a last goodbye, makes the final parting seem incomplete, cold, abrupt.

People are often stuck in grief when they have unfinished emotional business with a dearly departed. Sometimes, journalling helps. What would your last words be, was there anything you wanted to ask but couldn't? Writing it all down helps.

Matters of the heart are very complex, especially at the time of closure. Often, in our practice, I hear people pleading to get that "one audience" to be able to have that last conversation, the "last good bye", or work out unresolved issues. Alas, the universe allows only so much!

Counsellors, psychologists, therapists, from all over the world have reported that the number of distress calls have gone up considerably during the pandemic.

Handling grief after the demise of a loved one is not easy. Self-care is essential. The body, mind and soul need to be nourished. Extreme and prolonged stress can result in inflammation in the body. Stress is the root cause of many diseases. Continued stress can be fatal. It is, indeed, a condition not to be taken lightly.

Learnings:

1. After losing a loved one, get into a routine as soon as possible, however mundane it may be.

2. Any physical activity is helpful as it produces serotonin, the feel-good hormone, naturally uplifting the mood. Yoga and/or regular gym workouts will help.

3. If possible, travel, get away from familiar haunts and memories. Distractions help.

4. Engage and surround yourself with people who empathise with your emotions and are aware of your fragility at this time.

5. Research on nutrition and mental health has thrown up many foods considered to be mood lifters. Few of them are nuts, seeds and dark chocolates. Best to consume plenty of them if they suit your system.

6. It may be a good idea to have a companion animal as pet. They can love without judgement.

7. Professional counselling and medical help, if the situation gets out of control, is necessary.

8. Spirituality and religion can offer a balm to the soul.

LOVE, DEATH AND BEYOND

"What sets you apart can sometimes feel like a burden and it's not.
A lot of the time, it's what makes you great."
- Emma Stone

It's always a delight when you suddenly come across a unique combination of unassailable human spirit and emotional depth, someone who refuses to tread the beaten path. They are the true movers and shakers, who take every kind of risk to hew this adventure called life on their own terms. You are awestruck by their indomitable spirit, determination and resilience. They become the theme song of folklore for generations to come.

Lata and Lalit belonged to a small village in Eastern India where caste and community ruled the hearts and minds of the land. Fights ensued over tiny issues like your cow grazing in an unallotted slot in the open, to your cycle parked close to the gate of someone's home. Any crime more serious could involve the entire village. A verdict would be arrived at leisurely, depending on the mood of the *panchayat*, a village council, invariably headed by self-serving men who allowed a number of extraneous considerations to prevail over their judgement.

Lata needed to talk to someone, and that's when she made contact with us. She had suddenly lost her husband/partner/soulmate of 20 years and was emotionally distraught. She wanted to share her life story, and find answers, if any, for the way forward.

Her story unravelled over a few months during the lockdown; a story fascinating, absorbing and resplendent with electric moments. Her emotions were tangible as she relived the years, while recounting her tale of love.

Both Lata and Lalit grew up in a village, went to the local school and later, attended college in the nearby city. Since the college was 12 km away from her village, Lata had to travel by the state-run bus service. It took her half an hour each way given the condition of the roads.

She topped the XIIth standard board examinations and opted for further studies. Her school principal visited her home and convinced the family to allow her to pursue higher studies, as she would definitely secure a scholarship on academic merit. This helped tremendously as the family was struggling to make both ends meet. She had a younger brother who also attended the village school, but was not academically inclined. He would hang around with the other village boys and idle his time away.

In the rural tracts of India, the caste system plays a definitive role. Lata was from a lower caste and certain areas in the village were taboo for her caste. She felt claustrophobic in that setting. Intelligent and well-read, she envisaged a better life for herself, far from her current circumstances, where she would be treated on par with others.

Lalit belonged to the upper caste and was the son of a respected landlord in the village. He was privileged, good-looking and confident. He used to travel to other cities with his family for holidays or social engagements, so was exposed to progressive ideas.

Lalit used to cycle alongside Lata's bus everyday to college, and slowly, over a period of time, their eyes met and love blossomed. The curriculum was not varied so both of them had to choose common subjects. In the closed village setting, this gave them a good excuse to meet.

Despite the circumstances, their love story blossomed. But the differences in their caste and social status made it impossible to meet openly. Love, of course, would be out of the question. So their romance flourished discreetly, privy only to their shadows.

Lata had heard Lalit speak in debates and was very impressed with his progressive ideas and aversion to class, caste and other regressive societal values. Lalit grew fond of Lata's reserved and simple attitude, as she was mostly submerged in her studies and had no time for frivolous pursuits. She was a serious person, with a maturity far above her years. This impressed him.

Lata spent most of her time in the library and never in the canteen, which was actually a small outlet under a tree, selling tea and samosas. "I am petite and can be lost even in a small gathering of ten people," she admitted. "But Lalit noticed me and extended his hand of friendship. I resisted it in the beginning, thinking this relationship could go nowhere. But Lalit persisted and I eventually succumbed to his attention and charm.

Her voice, which expressed fear till now, suddenly had a lilt to it as she remembered the beautiful unending days of romance. Lalit would leave his home before the scheduled arrival of the bus, wait just outside the village, hide his cycle behind a tree and board the bus. They would talk about everything under the sun and beyond, holding hands and hoping the bus would take eternity to reach their destination.

"The great thrill was to meet every day and spend time together," she recalled. "The fear of being caught added to the adrenaline charge." Lata revealed that since Lalit was from an affluent home, the bus conductor wouldn't charge him for his ticket. "Such was the respect and fear for the upper caste."

Reliving the halcyon days, Lata continued, "One of our favourite discussions was about the social system and how unfair it was. Lalit was convinced that the situation would change, though at a slow pace. But we both decided not to bring children into such an imperfect, discriminatory, unequal world. We dreamt of a socially conscious, fair and equal world for all. We wondered when that would happen, if at all."

Time flew by and they reached the final year of college. With no other institute in the vicinity for further studies, how would they ever meet in the constricting social milieu they lived in? Lata's family had already started to scout for a groom for her and she was really nervous, as her love for Lalit was now a lifetime commitment.

After a lot of deliberation, the lovebirds decided to elope. They were sure about their death warrant if they disclosed their love to their families. There was an incident in the village a few years back when both the boy and girl were made to do a penance and then forced to marry someone else, as dictated by the panchayat. Luckily, they were not killed!

"Thus started our journey in the new life and an unending adventure," chirped Lata, recalling the early days. "We were both just 20 years old when we decided to elope. I had no money and it was left to Lalit to organise things and work out the details. I am 40-years-old now and what happened then seems like another incarnation.

"Lalit was confident that Dharmendra, his cousin in Delhi, who was teaching in a college, would help. I travelled by train for the first time in my life and was absolutely overawed by the journey, and Delhi." Dharmendra gladly provided them boarding and lodging. "The step we had taken was unheard of, and Dharmendra was happy to help, although a little scared. We started looking for jobs, but couldn't find any as both of us were only graduates, and didn't know spoken English well. We were keen not to burden anyone, so Lalit took up a job at a construction site as a daily wage worker. Although it was tough, our joy knew no bounds when he brought home his first wage. I remember, all three of us went to

Connaught Place and treated ourselves to special chaat."

As time passed, the situation turned critical. "Our joy was short-lived," continued Lata. "Our families had guessed what had happened and began hunting for us in earnest. Dharmendra decided that it was not safe for us to remain in Delhi, especially in his house, as the search party would land up there for sure. He requested another friend to accommodate us for a few weeks. It worked well. I helped in the housework there, and we contributed financially too. But two months later this friend's marriage was fixed by his family and so began our journey of finding another place to stay."

They seemed to be perpetually on the run. "Our next stop was Hyderabad, which was quite different from any other experience. Dharmendra sent us to friends, a young married couple. Pranav and Shubhra were happy to accommodate us. But before that, with Dharmendra as our witness, we sealed our relationship with marriage vows and the *saat pheras* in a temple. This seemed necessary for practical reasons. Though our souls were already married, our relationship needed legitimacy in the eyes of society. We started taking one day at a time as we had no road map. Everything was fluid and uncertain. Our big solace was that we were still together, and madly in love."

A new chapter began in Hyderabad. "Pranav, who ran a call centre of his own, helped Lalit secure a clerical job. He also persuaded us to learn spoken English, which was vital to procure a decent job. Shubhra was home-bound and more than happy to teach us English. I studied in earnest and picked up the language soon."

They also kept in touch with events back home. "We would speak to Dharmendra frequently to update him about our lives and also to get information about our families back in the village. He made a special trip to tell my family about my welfare and swore them to secrecy. They were relieved and happy that I had made a life for myself, far away from the constraints of the village. The villagers had guessed that we had eloped, since we both went missing at the same time. But the sin and stigma of inter-caste elopement remained with us throughout the years Lalit and I spent together."

Hyderabad exposed Lata and Lalit to new thought processes. They were on the run, in survival mode, and did everything legitimate to survive. "We realised that we could earn and live without having full-time jobs," explained Lata. "We got exposed to a number of ventures where we could get two meals and a place to sleep at night. There were plenty of religious places where you could volunteer and be provided with food and shelter. It opened our eyes to a world we had never known, and we embraced this world with arms wide open."

In a dreamy voice she continued, "We were not looking for any material security as most people do. We had each other, that was enough. We never thought of having a child. We were happy living like nomads. No commitment to the material, no house of our own, not many belongings and complete surrender to the Divine. We moved from one place to another, and never felt the need to live any other way."

The peripatetic life of travel and zero attachment continued. "After the first few years of finding our comfort zone, the next 15 years flew by. We travelled all over, lived and worked in churches, old age homes, social organisations, NGOs, religious shrines and earned enough to meet our needs. We never stuck to one place for more than a year. We were committed, hard workers, and so parting was always difficult. The organisations we worked for didn't want us to leave, but we were bitten by the travel bug. Life was beautiful and we had no regrets. But God had other designs."

Lalita's voice quivered as she relived that day. "We were travelling from Mysore to Kerala by road. On the way, Lalit went to relieve himself in a secluded area. It was dark and he did not see the snake. He must have accidently stepped on it. When he didn't return for a long time, we decided to take a look. We rushed him out of the forest but nothing much could be done as we were in the middle of nowhere. I lost Lalit to a snake bite!"

She lamented, "He has left me all by myself in this world, after making all those promises of living together forever. I sometimes feel like going back to the village but I have changed as a person, and don't want to put my family in trouble. Moreover, they may not accept me back."

In one of her calls, she talked about going to some ashram and settling down. Her parting sentence still haunts, "Now I have no one in this world. Can I call you sometimes just to talk?" Of course, we said, call any time, we are family.

Lata called again after a month to tell us about her new abode – an ashram where she has decided to do *seva* and spend the rest of her life. She added with a sigh, "I never felt the need to talk to someone all these years, but somehow I feel a sense of belonging after talking to you." As always we assured her of our availability, anytime she needed it, while wishing her the best for her new life's journey.

Learnings:

1. Parts of India still practice a rigid caste divide. One way to overcome the situation is education, as Lalit did in this case, and went ahead to embrace a life of love and happiness.

2. Some amount of divine grace and belief can work to your advantage.

3. Lata had lost Lalit at a young age, but she had lived a rich, fulfilled life. It may not have had material abundance, but it was definitely emotionally rewarding.

4. The ability to believe in yourself gives you the courage to fight and change the accepted norms of society.

5. Money has its uses but, as they say, the best things in life are free. Also, love conquers all!

YOUNG LOVE AND COVID-19

DATING IN COVID-19 TIMES

"Dating is about finding out who you are and who others are.
If you show up in a masquerade outfit, neither is going to happen."
- *Henry Cloud*

In the practice of mental health, the most common emotional issues we get to deal with are anxiety, relationships, marital problems, grief, loss of a loved one, the trauma of parenting, sickness, loneliness, alienation, addictions and so on. But the COVID-19 pandemic highlighted a totally new dimension in relationships, particularly the millennial dilemma of dating and intimacy.

With masks and social distancing made mandatory, newlyweds and dating couples were the worst hit. While the online and offline dating culture in India has been thriving, the millennial generation, which has been extremely active on the scene, is unable to decide the way forward.

Many young couples felt cheated as they were unable to take their relationship forward. Others felt that valuable time was being wasted, and then there were those who felt relieved that they now had a good excuse to distance from the relationship, and make a clean break.

Ashok joined college a year back. He was tall for his 17 years, well-built and handsome. Even as he was finding his feet in the new surroundings, he decided to date a girl he liked in his class. Ankita, at 16, was quiet, tall, fair and smart. They had met a few times just before the lockdown. He liked her and wanted to prospect the relationship.

"I am so upset with the situation now as there is no way to meet her," he complained. "How can we begin to know each other if we don't get to meet? We talk on the phone and sometimes video call but it is difficult to hold a conversation for long as we hardly know each other. We are unfamiliar with each other's likes and dislikes and there are awkward silences sometimes, as we don't know what to say. Even if I joke or say something silly, I could be misunderstood." He acknowledged this to be the new normal, but rued the loss of valuable time.

Ashok had time on his side. He was aware that he needed to meet many girls before deciding on "the one". Marriage was not on the cards yet.

"Identifying the right person is not a joke," he conceded. "My elder brother hasn't been able to find someone as yet and may have to settle for an arranged marriage. But it is such a passé thing, so old-fashioned to have an arranged marriage. All my friends will make fun of me. I would certainly prefer to find my own partner."

At *HalloHappiness* we explained that this new normal will also pass. Patience will be rewarded. It is all a process, and nothing remains stagnant. Meanwhile, we added, that cultivating a few good friends during the pandemic should be the way forward. Engage with similar mindsets. New friendships born in this period may culminate in something more promising. Ashok agreed. He found the conversations useful and promised not to be disheartened.

Learnings:

1. The new normal demands adaptability and resilience to act after understanding the situation.

2. Ashok is young and naturally impatient. Some guidance from the elders in the family would go a long way to assuage his fears.

3. It is important to understand the fears of the partner, as the girl may have other ideas about conducting the relationship.

4. Time alone will show the way forward as people are adapting, on a daily basis, to this new situation.

THE DEMISE OF INTIMACY

"When you are 29-years-old and haven't found the right girl to marry, it's a lot of pressure on your mind," confessed a worried Anmol. Sometimes, he worried if something was not quite right with him as the two girls he had dated, left him. He was very keen to start dating again.

"But what can I do in the lockdown? How do I date?" he sounded anxious. "Finding a date is not a simple process at my age, as I need to socialise, which is not happening now. I have sleepless nights wondering what the future of dating will be like. It is not fun holding a girl's hands with gloves, and you can't even see her face clearly through a mask. Will a normal physical date be a reality anymore? Will Corona ever have an exit date?"

Anmol was in a talkative mood. Being counsellors, we encouraged him to get his fears and apprehensions off his chest.

"It's scary," he continued. Anmol felt the COVID-19 story was here to stay. "There are so many versions everywhere, it's confusing. Work From Home (WFH) is also creating anxiety as you seem to be operating between four walls with no outlet of any kind. It is claustrophobic. How long can you hang around in the balcony and believe you are on a picnic? Meanwhile, I am trying to relax by listening to good music and practising yoga, my newfound love. That is until I find the real love of my life."

Dating, despite all the complexities, insecurities and dangers, is normally a pleasurable experience. A little anxiety is natural, especially if you are dating for the first time. In unprecedented times like these, it is quite natural for the youth to feel lonely, scared, uncertain and desperate about lost time. Besides, physical proximity has its dangers, what with the fear of getting infected.

Youngsters are unable to articulate their emotions and concerns to family members in these troubled times, fearing they may sound silly and trivial. This leads to further uncertainty, insecurity and misunderstandings.

Not meeting your partner is probably a little more challenging in our culture, where the pressure to get married at 'the right time' still remains strong. The needs of the youth are often trivialised. Successful dating and falling in love are a process of self-discovery. It necessitates falling in love with yourself first. But try explaining that to youngsters on hormonal overdrive!

The process of dating and finding that right partner for life involves several factors. At a younger age it is probably a little more complicated, since you are not sure of your own emotions and settling down is not a priority. Hormones and peer pressure add to the urgency. The maturity to understand patience and complex emotions like love are absent. Lust can overrule matters of the heart. It can easily turn volatile too.

Physicality can be a natural progression but a 'physical' date seems to be a far-fetched reality in COVID-19 times. As a result, our latent anxieties and uncertainties around dating, companionship and close relationships have resurfaced. Love in the time of COVID-19 has been hit as badly as the economy.

Intimacy need not necessarily mean a sexual relationship. While one can boost the other, it need not include the other. Intimacy involves trust, acceptance and an emotional connect with the other person. Intimate partners care for each other and are not afraid to share their thoughts, desires and vulnerabilities. Intimacy helps reduce stress and stay healthy. It counters loneliness and reduces the risk of mortality.

If you feel complimented, loved and appreciated, what more do you need? As it is often said, love and fresh air are all that are needed to be happy. But, right now, both are in short supply. It is well-documented that lack of love, isolation and stress have a negative effect on health. In COVID-19 times, as is quite evident, one's health may be battered by more than just a virus!

Learnings:

1. It is advisable to exercise patience. Try to identify your emotions and ensure that you get through this period with a positive outlook. There is no point fretting about the future.

2. When the time comes, your heart will identify the right course of action.

3. Times have changed and one has to adapt. Nothing lasts forever. Both good and bad times will run their course. So, make the most of the situation and, if need be, form your own rules for dating.

4. Whatever the situation, human beings have the resilience and enterprise to develop and flourish in a new normal. As a species, we have survived millennia. We will survive this too.

5. Keep a positive attitude always. Use the lockdown and isolation to learn new activities. Go within and begin another rewarding journey. Use the time well. It is fleeting.

LOVE, COVID-19 AND AN ANTI-CLIMAX

"You have given them unconditional love. They need to
know that even if they screw up, you love them. You don't want
them to grow up and resent you or, even worse, parent the way
you parented them."
- Alfie Kohn

There is something to be said about the young adults of our
country. They are extremely intelligent and, even if they are not
exceptionally well-read, they are equipped with all the information
they need from Google. They are masters at technology and can
change the world with the touch of a button.

Adept at making important life decisions, they ride high on ego and
confidence. Whatever they lack from limited human interaction
does not limit or constrict them in any way. They may be bereft
of the empirical knowledge of the previous generation, but that
doesn't deter them from taking major, even impulsive, on-the-spot

decisions. With the influx of technology in our lives, the world has become a village. Nothing really can limit you if you don't want it to. Today's generation is riding the crest of that gung-ho wave.

Alina was in the final year of her management studies and was eagerly looking forward to a working life after completing her studies. Although not good-looking in the conventional sense, her dusky complexion and smart carriage attracted a lot of admiring looks. Her confidence and clarity in her goals gave her a further edge. In short, she was much sought after.

Alina was in a relationship in college, had gone through a break-up, and was a regular caller for some time. The break-up shook her. She hadn't expected it since all seemed fine between her boyfriend and her. She was a smart girl, from an upper-class background, and life had been kind so far. But her boyfriend's non-responsive attitude towards her had caused a lot of anxiety, even thrown her into grave depression.

"This is the first time I am talking to some unknown person regarding a personal matter," she hesitatingly admitted. "I am feeling so unsure. It seems so strange to do this." We encouraged her to talk freely, no holds barred, and assured her that it would be completely confidential. We also explained that letting it all out would only heal her and help her come to terms with what had happened.

She understood, co-operated with us and opened up. We told her, in no uncertain terms, that a break-up wasn't the end of the world and the sooner she snapped out of it, the better.

Convinced, Alina started reworking her life. Soon, her calls reduced and finally stopped completely. Alina seemed mature, determined and positive. She seemed fully capable of reinventing herself, which she did.

In February 2020 Alina approached us again. She wanted to chat at night, which was fine by us, as a lot of our callers preferred late-night conversations. This was probably their private time at home.

"Here I am again," she started with a short laugh. She didn't say much and when we asked her if she wanted to discuss something important, her response was a bland, "I don't know." She disconnected after the short chat. We could sense that she wanted to say something but didn't know how to start. We hoped that she would call again.

A few days later, Alina did call. "You see, I am in love with a boy and as such there is no problem. He is 26 and I am 22 and we know our minds. This is not an adolescent love story as we are both mature adults." She continued after a pause, "He has a job but the problem is that I belong to a reasonably well-off business family, while he is from a poorer background, and my parents think that he is after my money and doesn't really love me. You know the usual bit about protecting me and all that." We asked her how long had they known each other. "Six months," she replied, sounding a little defensive.

She had approached us primarily to validate her plans to travel to Singapore for a week to surprise Sameer, her boyfriend, who was working there. She also thought that it may be an opportune time to test their feelings and check if they could take their relationship to the next level. It seemed like a good idea. "But I will have to give my parents some excuse for being away for a week as I can't disclose my plans to them," added Alina. "They would never understand."

We gently told her that lying to her parents was not on. That it was an act of deceit and was not conducive to a healthy parent-child relationship. But Alina seemed determined to go ahead with her plans. She called again and we reiterated that travelling out of the country to meet someone without informing her parents was not a great idea, and that she may want to reconsider or make alternate arrangements to meet Sameer. Her flighty, "I will let you know when I decide", did not sound convincing. But we hoped and prayed that she would drop her travel plans, make some other arrangement, or at least confide in someone in the family before embarking on the journey.

Then COVID-19 and the lockdown happened, and the world had other plans.

Alina's frantic call on March 22, 2020 was from Singapore. She had landed there on a Friday evening, to surprise Sameer at home and spend the weekend together with him. Instead, she was the one who was shell-shocked. Sameer had another girl in his apartment!

Alina hadn't expected this, even remotely. She also didn't have enough money to leave and check into a hotel. So, she was stuck. Sameer, meanwhile, packed off the other girl in a jiffy and tried to convince Alina that she was just a friend and there was nothing serious between them. "I am in a foreign country and I get lonely sometimes," he explained. "She is just a colleague visiting."

Alina had gotten over a failed relationship earlier and so her mind raced to the worst conclusions. She couldn't help feeling that Sameer had possibly betrayed her trust and love.

The weekend passed with both of them fighting. She had decided to fly back in two days on a very expensive return ticket since it seemed futile continuing to stay there.

But COVID-19 struck and a lockdown was declared. There were no flights to India as there was a travel ban and all the airports were shut. Alina was stuck big time.

Her biggest worry was the deception under which she had travelled, and her inability to explain her prolonged absence to her family. "What do I tell them about where I am, and how I cannot return home in a hurry even if I want to?" she cried. "I really can't give any excuse for being here. Besides, I don't know how long the lockdown will last and when I will be able to travel." Alina was panicking and rightly so. Not telling her parents was beyond all boundaries of family trust. She may have pulled it off if the lockdown hadn't happened. But now there was no escape from a candid confession.

We could empathise with her predicament but reiterated that the only way out was to come clean with her parents before the situation got murkier. "If I tell them I am with Sameer I will have no choice but to marry him, which I definitely don't want to now," she protested. We convinced her that the parent-child bond was sacrosanct and that it may be difficult to convince family members, but certainly not impossible. In the end, parents would always stand by their child. We persuaded her to speak to some friendly, older relative, who may enjoy the confidence of her parents, and would be able to convince them of the situation she was in.

Finally, after three long months, Alina took the first flight out of Singapore.

But the long story, with its ups and downs, had a silver lining. Sameer could prove his love for Alina, and they decided to get married.

It was, after all, a happy ending.

A positive outcome of COVID-19.

Learnings:

1. Due to a variety of reasons, children often do not understand the value system that parents want them to imbibe. It is done in the best interests of the child but, invariably, there is a miscommunication, misunderstanding and non-acceptance.

2. Sometimes, children are also limited in their understanding of life as they face a lot of peer pressure and are confined, and also defined, by it. They have to dare and bare, in a sense, or they may be labelled as sissies. At a certain age, it is vital to belong; to be a part of the brat pack.

3. The one thing every child needs to know and remember throughout his or her life, is that parents have unconditional love for them, and would be forgiving of their actions under most circumstances.

4. Parents, on the other hand, need to go out of their way to convince children of their unconditional love for them. There has to be free and open dialogue. Secrets are born in mistrust and distrust. As we know, open communication is the key to any healthy relationship.

5. Parents also need to 'chill', to put it in today's lingo. They need to understand that life has changed dramatically in recent times, with the introduction of technology. They have to adjust to changing circumstances and not sit in judgement with long-outdated values. Social reference points are not the same anymore. More than their children, parents have to evolve and accommodate new thought processes. A more liberal, global air has swept the land with its own consequences. Welcome to the new world!

ONLINE EDUCATION – BOON OR BANE

EDUCATION ANGST IN COVID-19 TIMES

"The goal of early childhood education should be to activate the child's own natural desire to learn."
- Maria Montessori

Modern education in India steers toward schooling from a very young age. The emphasis is on classroom learning geared towards high examination scores. This, unfortunately, is the main yardstick of scholastic excellence. We have heard stories of parents trying to get their unborn children admitted to the best schools. As they get older, quite naturally, the best institutes are chosen for higher education. This standardised system of education limits the free-spirited child. As is often said with some amount of truth in it, "school ruined my education". To quote Mark Twain, "Education consists mainly in what we have unlearned."

According to psychologists, the human brain grows the most between the ages of one and five years. So, when should one start formal schooling? Caught in the rat race, parents want to admit their kids to school as early as possible. With this, formal education begins early, and the kids get accustomed to some discipline. It also gives parents the freedom to pursue their careers. But is very early schooling a wise move?

Following COVID-19 and the evident risks involved in sending children to regular school, technology has been hailed world-over for saving the day.

The duration of an average class for this age group is 30 minutes to an hour. This isn't a long time, but children at that age do not have the patience or attention span to focus even for a few minutes. They love activity and getting them to sit still and focus for an online class is a nightmare for parents who are also on WFH (Work From Home) mode.

"From the time he has started online classes his attention span is barely five minutes at a time," complains Harshita, 4-year-old Harshil's mother. "When he attended school physically, he loved playing and running around with the other kids. It was an energising activity for him and also, thankfully, tired him out. He can't understand the concept of sitting across the screen. So, every now and then, he runs to get his toys and plays while sitting for his classes."

She also feels guilty about the extra screen time for Harshil. "Ironically, before the lockdown, he was allowed only one hour of onscreen play every day. Now, he is forced to attend online classes for almost three hours. After his classes, he wants to play computer games and throws tantrums if he is not allowed to. When he was attending play school, he had two hours of physical activity. But now since everything is online, he needs to get physically tired too to sleep easily."

With masks, social distancing and schools shut, online education became the only alternative. This brought about a fresh perspective in the education system, especially for pre/playschool-going children. According to WHO, children up to the age of six are best off with one hour of video/online interaction per day. But this shift from classrooms to online instruction has not been an easy transition for children aged three to five. They are too young to understand the implications, cannot sit focused for long and all they want to really do is play and have fun.

A paradigm shift in the schooling for toddlers may be needed keeping in mind future health risks and normal growth.

Learnings:

1. While the world has moved quickly to adapt to virtual life, children are finding it very difficult.

2. It might be worthwhile to explore other options like home schooling for them.

3. Alternatives are limited because going to a regular school provides all the ingredients for a healthy all round development in a child, absolutely necessary for well-rounded growth.

4. Beyond the pandemic, it might be prudent to evaluate the behaviour and mental health parameters of children. Symptoms like frequent crying, irritation, mood swings and withdrawal from social interaction, may be indications that all is not well. Communication and counselling may be required to address their fragile mental frame.

SOLELY ONLINE STUDY MAKES A DULL CHILD

"Technology is just a tool. In terms of getting the kids working together and motivating them, the teacher is the most important."
- Bill Gates

Four-year-old Namita attended a pre-school close to her home. It was convenient to walk to the school accompanied by her didi or the part-time domestic help. She had fun on the way, buying chocolates, nariyal pani and an odd flower for her teacher. Her mother was a working woman and dependent on the domestic help to look after her daughter.

All was well until COVID-19 and the lockdown happened.

Namita's parents were professionals and in WFH (Work From Home) mode. Meeta, her mother, was our client for some anxiety issues which were addressed and then her calls had stopped. When she called again after COVID-19, her anxiety levels were playing up as she was unable to keep her sanity intact.

With no help at home, multitasking was exhausting. Keeping up with Namita's classes was proving to be a nightmare. Namita, she explained, was always hyperactive. Sitting in one place and concentrating on the screen was a punishment for her. She used to enjoy walking to school as it was a much-needed exercise to her hyperactive personality. "Not only do I have to finish my office work, but I also need to make sure that food and snacks are available at the right time for everyone. I think of myself last, if at all. It is not just physically, but also emotionally exhausting," lamented Meeta.

Online education has several challenges. The teachers (it is all new for them too) are trying their best to manage the children online, by muting one child and allowing the other to speak.

Meeta complained that by the time Namita picked up an instruction, the teacher had moved on, since she couldn't actually monitor each child's activity or progress. As a result, Namita felt left out of most classes, which may have resulted in her losing confidence over a period of time.

"If she is made to sit down for long, she starts crying, demanding 'what kind of schooling this is?' How do I answer a four-year-old?" Meeta sounded frazzled. "So, we try to explain that this is only a temporary arrangement. Then I have no answer when she asks when she will be allowed to go back to the 'real' school." These questions are difficult for adults to answer, but innocent from a child's perspective.

It may not be a huge loss for a child to not attend school for a year. But the bigger challenge is for the parents, who are juggling many hats what with WFH, no support staff, housework, pressures in their jobs and personal relationships and no 'me time' or emotional buffer of meeting with friends and colleagues. Add to that monitoring their children during the online classes, taking up their studies and ensuring that they are disciplined, motivated and productively engaged.

Teachers too find it difficult coping with the new normal. Online teaching is as alien to them as it is for their wards. School allows interaction between teachers and children who need that guidance and support in their formative years. Children need positive, affirmative and healthy influences from adults other than their own parents. Teachers are the best early role models, as not many other adults are around in nuclear families. Besides being a platform for nurturing curious minds and building confidence, school is also an avenue for life skills where interaction with peer groups and a structured form of learning helps create capable adults.

What we are trying to teach today in play and pre-schools was something children learnt earlier, quite naturally and effortlessly in the joint family system, by observing family members. Cousins, uncles, aunts and even the old family servant could chastise the child if he or she went astray. It was a firm, solid support system.

Alas, all that is now lost to a generation living online!

Learnings:

1. While online education is not the best or permanent solution for this age group of children, a mix and match would probably be ideal in the long run.

2. To be able to attend school physically some days of the week and online schooling on other days might work well and provide the much-needed balance in kids' lives. The bigger challenge is to save children from getting infected while giving them a proper education.

3. Modern life is irrevocably moving towards an online existence. It will pose new challenges. The lockdown on physical activity is the first casualty. Alternatives will need to be explored to prevent the birth of an unfit generation.

4. Parents will need to be more creative in keeping their kids constructively engaged while retaining the fun element. Physical exercise at home could include skipping, yoga, playing within compounds with other children games like dodgeball, catch, badminton, cricket, running, walking and cycling. Some parents have even invested in inflatable pools which they pull out every once in a while for kids to splash around in.

THE WAY
FORWARD

LISTEN THROUGH YOUR EYES

"If we can share our story with someone who responds with empathy and understanding, shame can't survive."
- Brené Brown

While growing up, I remember being taught to speak, read and write but do not remember being taught to listen. I was sometimes asked if I was listening, but never told how to listen. There was great emphasis on handwriting, grammar, diction, pronunciation and elocution, but no one ever explained the art and importance of listening.

Listening is the missing half of communication. It is absolutely necessary in a conversation and is often overlooked. We are mostly 'hearing' but not listening. We are too distracted to listen. The 50-60,000 thoughts that pass through our minds every day clutter our heads. For active listening we need to declutter our minds. We have to listen to ourselves first.

We take listening for granted. In the guise of listening, we are actually biding time, thinking of our response. Active listening is something we need to practice. In genuine listening we can hear the underlying emotions of the speaker. We can hear the unsaid words.

Hearing is a natural act. Listening is a skill, and active listening builds trust. While listening, the three most important words are 'tell me more', which actually convey to the speaker that their story is important. It frees the speaker from the clutches of diffidence and insecurity and encourages thoughts and feelings to flow without encumbrance.

The other three very important words are 'what happened next?' It validates the speaker and prods him/her to open up. The process involves paying attention without judgement and interruption, an open posture, listening to really understand what is being said, interpreting the unsaid words and letting the information flow.

As a listener, you are working to impact the speaker. The first step to changing someone's thought process is to know what is in their minds. Listening is the missing key. It helps to connect. Everybody wants to be heard. That's why social media has become so popular in our lives. It helps people express themselves. Of course, honesty is not necessarily a part of social media and it is being hijacked by vested interests. But that is another story.

Three important reasons to listen:

1. It helps understand better the thoughts of the speaker. It is important in counselling as it helps change someone's thought process and, possibly, save a life.

2. It can establish a rapport with the speaker.

3. It helps open doors and facilitates easy exchange of ideas. It can help the speaker understand how wrong his or her thought process could be and makes room for remedies. By listening, we tune into the wavelength of the speaker and seek out what is not being said, as the core need is not often articulated.

In a conversation, we are normally thinking of an immediate response instead of listening. We judge a person in less than five minutes of being introduced. We look at people and the world with judgement. It is our perspective, totally individual, subjective and biased based on our personal experiences. The right open, non-judgemental perspective, however, can make the impossible happen. It can prevent conflicts between individuals, families, friends and work mates. And, if the conflict has already begun, it can help seek out solutions.

As a corporate counsellor, I get involved with conflict resolution very often. Sometimes it is individual and personal and, at other times, it crosses the boundary and involves family members or business associates. It is always interesting to observe the individual viewpoints and find a resolution.

An effective point of resolution has always emerged from taking a step back and analysing individual needs. Most times, it turns out to be very different from the actual conflict. Seemingly innocuous information, like a person's sun sign, can also come into play. It is not uncommon to hear a comment outside of a board room, right after a conclusive win-win situation, about an involved party's sun sign and why he/she can't be trusted. We do carry a lot of baggage!

I dream of a world of true and transparent communication. A world which produces more listeners than speakers. I would love a listening revolution. In the era of social media and so much clutter, it would indeed be true communication if someone was intently listening in to all the unexpressed emotions. It would be interesting to hold 'Listening Shows' instead of 'Talk shows'.

In my counselling experience, I have heard people identifying with an expressed emotion on social media and actually feeling better. Sometimes, people work out a solution for themselves and feel empowered. Solution finding may end up resolving a lot of individual conflict, creating happier marriages and happier children, with a better expression of love all around. Not everything will become pristine and hunky-dory but conflicts of all kinds – between parents, siblings and children, within relationships, marriages, organisations and maybe even nations – may peter down.

What an empowering thought!

THE JOURNEY

"If we can share our story with someone who responds with empathy and understanding, shame can't survive."
- Brené Brown

I was happy and content with my life and the work I was doing before I started *HalloHappiness*. I was keen to focus on "values I can add to other people's lives" and explore "what I can do to help other people". With *HalloHappiness* the world didn't change, but the way I looked at the world did. It changed my perspective.

HalloHappiness as a platform emerged much later. As far as I remember, I was always the 'go to' person for any emotional off-loading from family, friends or even professional colleagues. Not understanding 'textbook psychology', I often wondered about the small misunderstandings that led to big conflicts, and why nobody was 'listening' to the deeper emotions, crying to be heard.

We **started** the platform following WHO's philosophy of "Mental health for all by involving all", which originated from the acute shortage of professional psychologists or therapists for the number of people requiring support for mental health. Current estimate is about 400 million people worldwide.

We believe mental adaptability, more than physical endurance, will be the game changer in the future. At the top of that game will be the mental health and immune system of individuals. Happiness has been known to be the trigger for healthy minds and bodies, which builds up immunity.

At *HalloHappiness* we believe in every human being's right to a happy, wholesome experience of life, whatever the circumstances. We believe that a wholesome experience of life requires holistic well-being, combining mind, body and spirit, where mind is the initiator. We recognise the symbiotic relationship between them and consider all three while approaching any issue for counselling.

Our brain is like a computer, with compartments for: input, processing, output, hard disc and delete.

The hard disc carries all the processed input (memory). In life, invariably, there are certain experiences which are unpleasant. What's important is how that information is processed, and how it gets stored. Translated in the Indian system it is called *sanskara* (mental impressions) wherein the ultimate goal is not to hold on to or store the thoughts, impressions and experiences, as they form a part of our memory. One needs to become an onlooker and be free from them so they don't get carried over.

Your processor needs to identify the unpleasant experiences and store them in a zipped folder. Your brain may sometimes click on that zipped folder by oversight; the trick is to close it again, quickly. It is in such situations that *HalloHappiness* is a handy helping hand.

The processor is a unique part of the brain as it pretty much controls your reactions and monitors your perceptions which get stored in your hard disk (memory), if not deleted. It is quite complex as we still do not know for sure why two people react differently under the same/similar situations, why some people are unable to forgive/forget and allow those situations to dominate their lives and how some people are able to move on quickly.

One theory states that although we are born with a new brain and body, our intellect is inherited from the past. Trillions of cells in the body also carry their own memory, which combine with our present circumstances to establish our reaction. Our inability to handle any situation can be frequent, temporary or permanent and requires some external support to pass through the dark alley, which sometimes seems insurmountable.

At *HalloHappiness* we endeavour to provide you with simple tools, unique to your individual needs, and hold your hand to enable you to walk towards the light. Our experienced 'listeners' provide an empathetic ear to 'speakers', who want to offload their emotional trauma or distress to someone who would be non-judgemental. It heals to be heard.

Our focus group includes adolescents and teenagers, who are finding it very hard to communicate and need someone who can give them a patient 'listening'.

Disintegration of joint family systems, advent of nuclear families, uncertainties of life, unsaddled growth trajectory and societal approval all have contributed to the emotional build of today's adolescents and teenagers. We, as adults, are obliged to provide them a world full of emotional security and a positive outlook so that they can get a wholesome experience from life.

HalloHappiness conducts workshops and offers individual counselling, along with psychometric tests, to equip this vulnerable age group to have a complete and enriched life, emotionally and physically.

The struggle of parenting the millennial child has been an uphill task, and at *HalloHappiness*, one of our greatest accomplishments has been to forge a bond between parent and child through our simple techniques of psychometric tests and emotional counselling.

Most of our callers have heard about us through social media, the Rotary Club, homes for the elderly, educational institutes, PSUs and corporate workshops. Thus, adolescents, teenagers, couples, housewives and professionals have been drawn to our platform. Another vertical developed for the elderly, who needed some emotional support and engagement, has opened up. Some need upliftment from daily emotional upheaval, loneliness or support to overcome a sense of neglect.

Our experience shows that any physical ailment being treated in combination with emotional counselling, has resulted in at least a 20 percent benefit to the healing process. It also impacts the caregiver along with the patient.

The results have been exceptionally encouraging as in long-term treatments, patients lose hope and become depressed, especially in cases of physical restrictions. The mind is unable to register the effect of medication unless it 'believes' in a positive outcome. The resistant mind results in 'slow' or sometimes 'no recovery', as all sustainable impact originates from the mind.

We found that emotional counselling was especially beneficial in the recovery of patients who were bedridden with comorbidities, for a longer period of time, and who needed some emotional support to be motivated. We provided them the essential, initial 20 percent emotional motivation for the 'desire' for life, and to get better.

The frenetic pace of life has thrown logical thinking out of the window leading to social abuse, domestic violence and frequent family breakdowns. Being unappreciated is a common complaint of callers registering with us, leading to emotions of guilt, anger, frustration and sometimes even depression.

Personal sexual preference is now recognised as an individual freedom. However, emotional upheavals, especially in the youth, are quite distressing and a guiding hand from our empathetic counsellors goes a long way in settling those emotions.

As a corporate/business counsellor, I come across conflicts or stalemates which often have no substantial basis. In most cases, a lot of past emotional baggage clouds the judgement and complicates situations to become seemingly unresolvable.

In a particular case of separation in a business family, the unresolved issue turned out to be the ancestral home where the family was residing, which had been bought by their late father.

It has always helped to resolve such tricky emotional issues by stepping back. As 'listeners' we took that approach and engaged the grandchildren to provide a happy ending, as the elders were unbending about the deserving inheritor of the house.

Every single day has been a learning process for us and our endeavour to resolve emotional issues faced by our clients ultimately brings a smile to our face, and the enriching experience of finding THE solution in a given unique situation is our greatest reward.

We dream of a world full of happy minds and happier lives.

THE WAY FORWARD: IMMUNITY IMMUNITY IMMUNITY!

Our immunity plays a very important part in our well-being. Nobody from our generation anticipated COVID-19, but going by the worldwide history of past pandemics, viral infections in the future seem a definite possibility. Apart from the vaccine, the greatest differentiator has been the immune system of individuals.

Mental health plays a very important role in our immunity as happy minds have a better immune system. This being an invisible disability not measurable by a pathological test is highly underscored in our daily lives. Outcomes of stress, anxiety, depression and other mental health related issues are often attributable to external factors also.

Fortunately, there is help available. Your immune system has compartments that can be quantified and measured by a blood test. It can be strengthened gradually, to give you a better quality of life.

At *HalloHappiness* we provide evaluation of individual immune systems by first organising a blood test and then having immunologists on our panel suggest ways to strengthen your immunity. A periodic evaluation will be structured to offer outcomes with precision for your current state, and what will most likely be your future direction.

People who opted for our services for strengthening their immunity, experienced great improvement in their mental health, as improved immunity not only strengthens your system, it also provides motivation and a positive approach to life.

In German there is a term called doppelganger, which means 'friendly ghost'. Doppelgangers are those crucial friends in your journey of life that will protect you when you are a baby, run with you when you are an adult and slow down in your old age. More importantly, they will strengthen your physical responses when you are looking after your physical self, keep you mentally fit when you invest in your mental well-being and hold your hand when you have an injury, infection or are simply slowing down as a natural ageing process.

Your immune system is your doppelganger. It is the response your body has prepared against every trauma, insult or injury, mental or physical. A robust immune system will ensure that infections will pass you by without lasting damage, just as a weakened immune system will prolong physical infirmity, or invite mental ineptitude, including gloominess, despair, lack of initiative and interest or even depression and suicidal ideation.

The WFH (Work From Home) culture that has emerged due to the COVID-19 pandemic, has forced us to look at other emerging trends like the crucial role of technology. Before the pandemic, there was a movement on ways to cut down on the usage of gadgets due to their adverse effects. Apart from their impact on our own body and mind, they prove detrimental to the environment as well. Unfortunately, the future is probably going to be more technology and gadget dependent, and we definitely need to concentrate on optimum utilisation, as e-waste is a bigger menace for the environment.

Life is about reinventing, and man, adept at self-preservation, has certainly adapted to meet challenges time and again. From a world of consumerism and materialism, the pandemic brought humanity back to a minimalistic way of life, to find abundance within.

Here's looking forward to a world of balance. The normal.

IN CONCLUSION

We look forward to our request to the Government of India for the incorporation of NHI (National Holistic Happiness Index) in the GDP. If accepted, this would set a new trend as the NHI would take a holistic approach for measuring the happiness and well-being of the large and diverse Indian population. It could be a measurement tool and used for policy-making for enhanced NHI.

Before that, a nationwide implementation of such a declaration in the balance sheets of corporate India can be undertaken. Employees' surveys can be conducted on the parameters, and company policies can be adopted accordingly, as employee absenteeism, physical as well as mental, results in reduced productivity of the worker.

The current system is focussed on providing tools and measures to employees to be able to 'manage' mental health/happiness once detected on evaluation. The world has moved to preventive mode as the impact of economic cost is much higher in post-infirmity management. Such a survey, made mandatory, will be used for policy-making in an inclusive fashion, much as CSR has become a compulsory component for corporate India.

Say Hello to Happiness.

...ABOUT HALLOHAPPINESS

"The most beautiful people we have known are those who have known defeat, known suffering, known struggle, known loss, and have found their way out of the depths. These persons have an appreciation, a sensitivity, and an understanding of life that fills them with compassion, gentleness, and a deep loving concern. Beautiful people do not just happen".
- Psychiatrist Elisabeth Kubler Ross,
Source: Death-The final Stage of Growth

I quote from *Systems of Psychotherapy, A Transtheoretical Analysis,* Seventh Edition, by James O. Prochoska and John C. Norcoss. It lucidly explains the current state of therapies. No further explanation is required.

"The field of Psychotherapy has been fragmented by future shock and staggered by over choice. We have witnessed the hyperinflation of brand names of therapies during the past 50 years. In 1979, *Time* magazine was reporting more than 200 therapies. Recent estimates put the number at over 400 and growing.

"The proliferation of therapies has been accompanied by an avalanche of rival claims. Each system advertises itself as differently effective and uniquely applicable. Developers of new systems usually claim 80 percent to 100 percent success, despite the absence of controlled outcome research. A healthy diversity has deteriorated into an unhealthy chaos. With so many therapy systems claiming success, which theories should be studied, taught or brought?

"We believe that fragmentation and confusion in psychotherapy can best be reduced by a comparative analysis of psychotherapy systems that highlight the many similarities across systems without blurring these essential differences.

"No single definition of psychotherapy has won universal acceptance. Depending on one's theoretical orientation, psychotherapy can be conceptualized as interpersonal persuasion, health care, psychosocial education, professionally coached, self-change, behavioural technology, a form of reparenting, the purchase of friendship, or a contemporary variant of shamanism among others."

In counseling/therapy a major danger that can happen is of ignoring or minimizing social reality as we not only need sensitivity but also understanding. We do tend to have difficulty in dealing with people who are in some significant way different from us. We all hold views which have the potential to be discriminatory, prejudiced and exclusionary due to our past experiences. We need more of therapists, counsellors, life coaches, trainers and the like to consider and address such attitudes and behaviours in ourselves. Every individual is unique and our uniqueness defines as well as separates us.

This is where *HalloHappiness* steps in to make a difference.

HalloHappiness (an online confidential counseling service) is my brainchild and a tribute to my late mother. My earliest memories of my mother is someone who had anxieties and dealt with them the best she could. What we did not know was that her anxiety issues were caused by an imbalance in her thyroid glands. She had hypothyroidism, a treatable condition that went unnoticed for quite a while.

She did not choose to be anxious - it was a natural fallout. However, her rich, empathetic emotional built, in spite of her anxiety issues, made her a 'listener' for anyone who needed it. I don't know of any life that she touched who was not overwhelmed by her persona – dignified, aristocratic, generous and above all, of a non-judgmental disposition. She reinvented herself by writing short stories. She became an ideal 'listener'.

One of my siblings inherited anxiety issues from her, struggled for a number of years and finally overcame it by receiving counselling from me. People who can get that non-judgmental, confidential 'listener' within the family are lucky but most times outside help is needed as immediate circumstances/situation play a big role.

HalloHappiness existed in my mind throughout those years but fructified much later, as a platform for holistic living involving mind, body, spirit with emotional health at the centre of it all.

We combine ancient knowledge viz Yoga, Meditation, Pranayam and Sanskrit language known for its calming effect and developing a focused mind. Our sessions are prescribed after studying issues and requirements unique to an individual's body and mind. We provide evidence-based counselling that is effective, affordable and client centred to address common mental health issues like anxiety, depression, restlessness, loneliness etc. Our empathetic counsellors have combined experience of more than 5000 hours. We do not prescribe any medication or prescription drugs.

For more information, you can connect with us on:
Email: support@hallohappiness.com
Hallohappiness17@gmail.com
Tel: +91 9372159459
www.hallohappiness.com

www.ingramcontent.com/pod-product-compliance
Lightning Source LLC
LaVergne TN
LVHW090947180726
843490LV00001B/154